FOCUS ON REVELATION

A PRACTICAL LOOK AT REVELATION FROM A SINGULAR MECHANICAL PERSPECTIVE

BOB SMITH
EDITED BY SARAH BRYANT

Though the fig tree should not blossom, nor fruit be on the vines, the produce of the olive fail and the fields yield no food, the flock be cut off from the fold and there be no herd in the stalls, yet I will rejoice in the LORD; I will take joy in the God of my salvation. (Habakkuk 3:17, 18)

Published by

A Voice of One Ministries

Permission is granted to all to copy in part and distribute freely for the glory of the Almighty and one true God. Throughout this work all pronouns indicating either the Father or Jesus are capitalized out of respect for the Almighty One and His agent. Except where otherwise noted all scripture quoted is from the English Standard Version (ESV).

ברוף יהוה

TABLE OF CONTENTS

PREFACE	4
1 GETTING STARTED	9
2 E=THE DAY OF THE LORD	16
3 MOVING ON	24
4 THE SEVEN STEPS	31
5 THE FINAL THREE	43
6 FOREST FOR THE TREES	59
7 JOHN'S INTRODUCTION	62
8 THE SEVEN LETTERS	68
9 THE OVERTURE	77
10 THE 144,000 & THE GREAT MULTITUDE	79
11 THE ANGEL AND THE SEVEN THUNDERS	85
12 THE TWO WITNESSES	89
13 THE WOMAN & THE DRAGON	93
14 THE BEAST AND THE FALSE PROPHET	100
15 THE THIRD TEMPLE	120
16 CHAPTER FOURTEEN	133

17 SECOND OVERTURE	147
18 THE TALE OF TWO WOMEN	149
19 THE FALL OF BABYLON	157
20 THE SEVENTH STEP	164
21 THE DAY OF THE LORD	168
22 ALL THINGS NEW	175
23 CONCLUSION	177
24 CONCERNING DEATH	179
25 HELL	197
ILLUSTRATIONS	210
NOTES	212
INDEX	213

PREFACE

The book of Revelation is undoubtedly the most misunderstood book of the Bible. Volumes upon volumes have been penned upon it ranging from the technical to the fanciful. A great deal of writers candidly admit its clandestine and problematic nature, yet if you were to simply peruse many of the writings concerning it you would find no shortage of those who claim to know its brilliantly concealed secrets, some even being touted as "experts." As blatantly cocky as it sounds, I believe that I do possess the key to understanding the book, or rather was *given* it, and that the vast majority of books written on how to interpret it are built upon shaky foundations and are simply wrong. Furthermore, it is my assertion that the book when understood gives insight into understanding the total of God's work in this world; inversely, if you understand His plan for mankind then you will certainly be capable of understanding Revelation. This little work is intended for those, who through their willingness to accept the truth, are capable of receiving it. As Jesus said, "He who has ears let him hear" (Matthew 13:9). I have purposely taken a non-conventional approach in this writing in order to facilitate ease of learning; I deal with the structure first then go on to the particulars. I could easily repeat myself or drone on over minutiae that tend to confuse and disorient one from absorbing the basics, but how does that help anyone?

The Revelation as well as the Bible as a whole is actually a simple book to understand when it is interpreted from a single perspective. If you concentrate and focus upon one particular future event toward which everything in this present age is proceeding, then it all becomes crystal clear. That event is known as the Day of the Lord, and its importance to understanding God's plan for man cannot for our purposes be overstated. If you retain that fact in mind, then the book that men have struggled with for centuries can be made sense of in mere minutes.

At no time do I mean to say that I have all the answers to every detail of the book. My method of interpretation is concerned primarily with the structure of the book. Much of the Revelation is cryptically presented and is subject to opinion; mine may not always be 100% correct. The overall perspective and method of interpretation is sound, however, and the adoption of it is in my opinion the only way to make sense of the book. The book of Revelation is a *revealing* of God's plan for mankind and it is my firm conviction that He is using me to uncover many wondrous truths that are contained within it.

However, it is necessary that you have at least read the book and have a passing knowledge (however vague) of how it is constructed in order to gain much from my effort at teaching it. Therefore, if you are not familiar with it, put this down and become so first. If you are currently reading any commentary about Revelation then set it aside or better yet use it as door stop or window prop (just kidding).

Who am I and why should you listen to me? In a word I am nobody. I don't have a degree from a seminary, college, or online school. In all things Biblical I am self-taught, so either the following is a fabrication of a weak minded fool or the inspired truth that comes only through the Immortal Spirit; you decide. I initially apologize for my crude method of delivery of this material but not for its content. It is what it is. To you that read this regardless of my credentials, I assert that you are indeed holding in your hand a rudimentary and unassuming key to unlocking a hidden mystery that is centuries old. So for no one else's sake but your own, I implore you to slowly read, reflect, and consider what I have to offer.

By way of reference and in keeping with a commitment toward full disclosure, I am writing this from the perspective of a Biblical Unitarian; my creed is the Hebrew shema ("Hear O Israel YHVH is our God, YHVH is one") and I believe that there is but one God, the Father, and that Jesus is not God, i.e. a part of a trinity or a divine personage come down to earth, but is the Father's anointed human representative in this world. He is the primary agent of the Almighty One in this and the coming age and, as a result, is worthy of our worship. Additionally, I espouse a few doctrines that the average professing Christian will find strange, for some even heretical, but hold on to your horses before passing judgment and I hope to make that which is dark become light. It should also be noted that I employ aside from the scriptures a very limited bibliography; I consulted few other expositors in my studies. Any extra-Biblical facts I present are not included in the notes simply because such information can easily be verified through a quick internet or library search.

The following teaching began to enlighten me well over three decades ago. As a young man in the early 1970's, I first became aware of Bible prophecy through Hal Lindsey's book *The Late Great Planet Earth*. I was fascinated with the study of eschatology. However, it did not take me long to realize that I was totally confused when I read the book of Revelation against it. There were so many loose ends and unanswered questions regarding the subject that I understandably felt overwhelmed. I was, however, determined that I was going to find out the answers, so I began to study Revelation in earnest. A short while later (ca.1979) as a newlywed I was studying the book of Revelation one day in a Laundromat at an apartment complex where my wife and I lived. As she was busy washing and drying our clothes, I was sitting on a folding table reading a small, pink, vinyl covered New Testament (a New American Standard Bible) when the first of many times spiritual light began to illuminate my thoughts. It was one of those "Aha!" moments. Like the growth of a child it came in spurts over a period of several years, and now takes its' mature form that you'll see in these pages. This all began to come about as the result of simply asking God for it:

"If any of you lacks wisdom, let him ask God, who gives generously to all without reproach, and it will be given him. But let him ask in faith, with no doubting, for the one who doubts is like a wave of the sea that is driven and tossed by the wind." (James 1: 5, 6)

I highly recommend if you are to reap any benefit from this work that you follow suit and ask God for the wisdom that He only can give through His Spirit. However, be aware it only works if you truly desire to know the truth, so examine your heart and determine your intentions. Additionally, it would be most helpful if you try to forget anything you think you know on the subject until you have finished reading this, after which you can contact me at avoiceofone@earthlink.net with any questions.

GETTING STARTED

Many years ago I heard that famous radio preacher with the west Texas drawl, J. Vernon McGee, state that all books on Bible prophecy were carbon copies of one another. His point was that there is essentially nothing new being revealed in eschatology from that which other men have previously taught and written upon. In as far as premillienialists are concerned he was correct, those who adhere to the doctrine largely base their intrepretations on a literal chronological view, one which he held. Although our theologies are now miles apart, I've always had a great respect for McGee based upon his ministry of teaching God's word, yet I believe that he, as well as other premillienists, was wrong in his opinions on eschatology and intend to prove it in this current work. Let there be light.

It's universally conceded by most Biblical scholars that the book of Revelation is a cryptic puzzle that is to be interpreted, at least in certain places, allegorically. I must certainly concur that it is a puzzle, literally, and must be interpreted as such in order to be understood. Therefore, my approach is primarily mechanical; I deal with the book's structure. A jigsaw puzzle is an excellent metaphor in this regard. Over the years, I have assembled a few and had in the process an enjoyable time doing it. There are a number of ways to go about solving or assembling one, but invariably it is universally agreed by those who have worked on one that the easiest way is to start by building the outside edges first. Those pieces are readily recognized and, when assembled, create the form of the puzzle; its outer edge. Whether the form is rectangular, square, round or any other shape we find an initial ease of assembly simply by taking the outer pieces and assembling them according to its shape. The form itself tells you very little about the subject, it simply reveals its basic shape and outline, its limit, yet it must be recognized in order to proceed with the solving process, therefore the first point that I must emphasize is that THE FORM OF THE BOOK IS THAT OF A NARRATIVE. A narrative is read linearly, along a line from the start to the finish. This is where the vast majority of people interpreting the book go wrong; they attempt to understand it as a story by its form.

It is the content, however, in which the truth will be found, so forget about understanding it by starting at the beginning and working your way through it; that method just does not work. I have seen and heard men attempt to teach the book exactly like that on numerous occasions (too many to number) and, frankly speaking, they failed to bring much light to the darkness. In order to make sense out of it you must analyze and arrange the *elements within the book.*

It should be noted that the form of this commentary (though it's not actually a commentary; it's more of a primer) does exactly that; I address the subject matter of Revelation directly. I do not follow a linear path in deciphering its meaning, yet when understood, its significance will become all too apparent. The book is fraught with symbolism and allegorical imagery, not everything in the Bible should be taken literally; Jesus Himself taught in parables and for a reason:

"Then the disciples came and said to him, "Why do you speak to them in parables?" And he answered them, "To you it has been given to know the secrets of the kingdom of heaven, but to them it has not been given. For to the one who has, more will be given, and he will have an abundance, but from the one who has not, even what he has will be taken away. This is why I speak to them in parables, because seeing they do not see, and hearing they do not hear, nor do they understand." (Matthew 13:10-13)

The teaching concerning God's kingdom is purposely hidden in plain sight; figuratively speaking, it's under everyone's nose. Jesus, knowing man's soulish[1] nature, beckoned to His sheep by proclaiming "He who has ears, let him hear."(Matthew 13:9). This admonition is found in the synoptic gospels whenever He wanted His followers to pay strict attention (Matthew 11:15, 13:9, 43; Mark 4:9, 23, 7:16; Luke 8:8, 14:35). Perhaps it should come as no surprise that it is also found in the Revelation eight times (Revelation 2:7, 11, 17, 29; 3:6, 13, 22; 13:9)! The reason for this is obvious; He is telling His followers something very important.

But before you can deal with the different elements you need to recognize and understand the book's subject (that *single perspective* I mentioned in the introduction). How do we do that? Well, when building a puzzle the best way is to look at the picture on the box cover! Revelation has a clear subject.

On a wall in my home is a Snellen eye chart. This is the standard eye chart found in doctor's offices around the world. I keep and display it as a visual aid in reminding me that like the big "E" at the top of it is a focal point for the eyes, God too has a focal point in the time ages that all things in His revelation - the Bible - point toward. It is a point yet in the future when all things on this earth are destined to be brought toward and in which they find their culmination [fig.1]. It is the coming of God's kingdom on the earth. Another good illustration is found in a common everyday bathroom fixture, the bathtub. Put a drain plug in, fill it with water, and then pull the plug. Starting with a big gulp, the water will begin to rush toward the drain. The drain is like the Day of the Lord, everything in this age will rapidly move toward it once the event known as the Great Tribulation (the plug) initiates.

"making known to us the *mystery* of his will, according to his purpose, which he set forth in Christ *as a plan for the fullness of time, to unite all things in him, things in heaven and things on earth.*" (Ephesians 1:9, 10)

Paul here spoke of it as the mystery of His will. God's will is to unite everything in both heaven and earth under one King, Jesus the Christ. It is toward this end that all the prophets spoke about, that the promise to King David of an eternal kingdom was made, and is the subject of the parables of Jesus. It is in truth the big "E" toward which all things in this age must focus. In Revelation chapter 10 we find in narration its fulfillment:

"And the angel whom I saw standing on the sea and on the land raised his right hand to heaven and swore by him who lives forever and ever, who created heaven and what is in it, the earth and what is in it, and the sea and what is in it, that there would be no more delay, but that *in the days of the trumpet call to be sounded by the seventh angel, the mystery of God would be fulfilled*, just as he announced to his servants the prophets." (Revelation 10:5-7)

What is this Mystery, this focal point? It is the ushering in of the Day of the Lord, a particular future time spoken of by the Old Testament prophets, Jesus, and the Apostle Paul. THIS, YOU WILL SEE, IS THE VERY SUBJECT OF THE BOOK OF REVELATION. I CANNOT STRESS THIS SECOND POINT TOO MUCH. This is the "kingdom come" for which Jesus taught us to pray (Matthew 6:10).

John begins his "revealing" of the vision by stating this:

"I, John, your brother and partner in the tribulation and the kingdom and the patient endurance that are in Jesus, was on the island called Patmos on account of the word of God and the testimony of Jesus. I was in the Spirit *on the Lord's day*," (Revelation 1:9, 10)

Among some scholars the phrase in italics has been bandied about as to its exact meaning. Is it referencing a day of worship or a day of vengeance? The word day is not in the genitive case (the case which shows possession) but in the accusative (the direct object which indicates something concerning or pertaining to the subject). It is *Lord* that is found in the dative (case of the indirect object). It is not the normal form used to designate *that day*. My opinion is that although it is not named as such, the preposition concerning it is to be considered. The Greek preposition EN here translated as *on* is always governed by the dative case and means *in* or *among*. The preposition here is the key. John is saying that he was *in spirit in the Lord's Day*. The word Lord carries the definite article (the).

It must be taken into account that at no other place in the New Testament is there any mention of a Lord's Day as a day of worship or any other purpose, and to deem this one so is at best an assumption. There are some references to the first day of the week in the scriptures (Acts 20:7; I Corinthians 16:2) as a day of meeting, but no hint of a mandate for worship. The resurrection of Christ and the subsequent meetings with His disciples was also on the first day of the week, but, again, no clear mandate. I suspect that the linguistic emphasis here may be on John's position in that day.

So, what am I saying? Simply this, that the inclination to assume that day refers to Sunday, Saturday, or any other day of the week may be incorrect; the preposition tells us that John was present in spirit in the Lord's Day. It was as if he was present and had a front row seat to the events that are to take place in the future. It is my position that the day that pertains to the Lord is *His day of judgment* and is a reference to the Day of the Lord. This was the day that John found himself in while on the island of Patmos.

Let me sum it up here:

- The book is in the form of a narrative.
- The book is correctly interpreted by its content.
- The book has a clear subject, the Day of The Lord

- The Day of the Lord is the focal point toward which everything in this age moves. It is the conclusion of the Mystery of God's will, the picture on the box.
- The 10th chapter of revelation confirms it.
- John, the writer of Revelation, may have been in the midst of the Day of the Lord by virtue of the Spirit when he received the vision.

E= THE DAY OF THE LORD

What exactly is the Day of the Lord? Depending on whose teaching you follow, it varies. Some teach that it is a single 24 hour day. Others believe that it encompasses the seven year Tribulation period. The following is what I believe to be the correct doctrine. In order to understand it, we must have a clear definition of what is a day. Because the Bible, specifically the Old Testament which comprises approximately 75%, was written in Hebrew, we must therefore acquaint ourselves with the Hebraic concept and meaning of *day*. In other words, we must read it with Hebrew glasses. This is found in the first book of the Bible, Genesis.

"And God said, "Let there be light," and there was light. And God saw that the light was good. And God separated the light from the darkness. God called the light Day, and the darkness he called Night. And there was evening and there was morning, the first day." (Genesis 1:3-5)

Here we see the Hebraic definition for day; light is day, it begins with the evening, and goes from darkness into light; from the evening (Hebrew EREV) to the morning (BOQER). Even to this day, faithful Jews reckon the day to begin at sundown (EREV) and extend through the night, past the morning (BOQER) to the following sundown; it is a twenty four hour period.

The Hebrew itself bears this out; the word translated *first* is often done so incorrectly. In keeping with proper English grammar, most English Bible translations render the Hebrew ECHAD by the ordinal word *first*, which is incorrect. It rightly should be rendered by the cardinal word *one*, thus making it read "there was evening and there was morning, *one day*. This correct translation gives us a clear and unadulterated definition of what a day is, a period of light that proceeds out of darkness.

Throughout the Old Testament prophetic books there is a recurring theme concerning God's punishment of the nations of the earth (Isaiah 13:6, Jeremiah 46:10, Ezekiel 30:3, Obadiah 15, etc.). The Day of the Lord, or some facet of it, is mentioned in all the prophetic books except Jonah. You cannot read the Old Testament prophets and come away without addressing the subject matter of that day. It is a major theme found throughout the Old Testament, one that can't be ignored.

"Enter into the rock and hide in the dust from before the terror of the LORD, and from the splendor of his majesty. The haughty looks of man shall be brought low, and the lofty pride of men shall be humbled, and the LORD alone will be exalted ***in that day***. For the LORD of hosts has a day against all that is proud and lofty, against all that is lifted up--and it shall be brought low." (Isaiah 2:10- 12) (Bold italics mine)

Here is a great example of how the Day of the Lord is expressed in scripture: Though not specifically named as such, it is clearly indicated in the phrase "For the LORD of hosts has a day". This is done throughout Isaiah. There is coming a time when God will have had enough of man's disobedience and he will bring together all the parts of His plan.

But the vengeance of the Almighty One is just an initial part of that day; references abound about other occurrences that appear to be contradictory to a day of vengeance. This is because the Day of the Lord is actually an age rather than a 24 hour period. It is a thousand years long day that is also an age. The Apostle Peter was explicit in regards to that day:

"But do not overlook this one fact, beloved, that with the Lord one day is as a thousand years, and a thousand years as one day. The Lord is not slow to fulfill his promise as some count slowness, but is patient toward you, not wishing that any should perish, but that all should reach repentance. But the day of the Lord will come like a thief, and then the heavens will pass away with a roar, and the heavenly bodies will be burned up and dissolved, and the earth and the works that are done on it will be exposed." (II Peter 3:8-10)

Notice that the phrase *The Day of the Lord* follows on the heels of his statement that *one day is as a thousand years with the Lord.* That particular verse has been taken out of context so often by so many, but don't be fooled, it is referring to the Day of the Lord. If you read the 3rd chapter of II Peter and consider its meaning, you will see that the entire chapter is about the things that the prophets of the Old Testament predicted. Peter ended the letter with words that indicate that the Day of the Lord is in fact an age:

"But grow in the grace and knowledge of our Lord and Savior Jesus Christ. To him be the glory both now and to the day of eternity. Amen." (II Peter 3:18)

I've often wondered if those who worked on the modern translations such as the English Standard Version were either unaware or troubled at how to translate the phrase "day of eternity" which literally means *unto (the) day age*. In almost all translations the word AEON (age) is rendered there as *eternal, eternity, forever*, or a variant thereof which obscures the meaning of the text. The word that is commonly rendered (incorrectly) as *eternal* or *everlasting* is AIONIOS the adjective form of the Greek AEON (age) used above. In the English language when a noun pertaining to time is used as an adjective the suffix –ly is added; thus hour becomes *hourly*, day becomes *daily*, month becomes *monthly*, etc. But the noun age does not have an adjectival equivalent; there is no such word as *agely*. I'm certainly no grammarian, but even I can see that by taking an undefined noun and making it a much defined adjective as in this case is wrong. The word AEON as used here should be rendered as *age* not *eternity*. What Peter wrote was that the Day of the Lord was indeed an age and a day of a thousand years – the Kingdom age. Compare the above quotation from the ESV to Anthony Buzzard's translation:

To him be the glory both now and for the future age-long day. Amen. (The One God, the Father, One Man Messiah Translation)

So now you may be thinking, "Hey! You said that a day is defined as light!" And indeed I did. How is it possible to reconcile these two things, light and a thousand year period? God gives us the answer near the beginning of the book of Isaiah. *That day* is defined by a great light that appears over Jerusalem:

"*In that day* the branch of the LORD shall be beautiful and glorious, and the fruit of the land shall be the pride and honor of the survivors of Israel. And he who is left in Zion and remains in Jerusalem will be called holy, everyone who has been recorded for life in Jerusalem, when the Lord shall have washed away the filth of the daughters of Zion and cleansed the bloodstains of Jerusalem from its midst by a spirit of judgment and by a spirit of burning. Then the LORD will create over the whole site of Mount Zion and over her assemblies *a cloud by day, and smoke and the shining of a flaming fire by night*; for over all the glory there will be a canopy. There will be a booth for shade by day from the heat, and for a refuge and a shelter from the storm and rain." (Isaiah 4:2-6)

This cloud and flaming fire is reminiscent of the shekinah glory (presence) that proceeded before the children of Israel and stood above the tabernacle when they traveled in the wilderness for forty years (see Exodus 13:21, 22). In fact, it appears to be the very same thing, the very presence of God made visible. Now, envision that this flaming fire is a bright light that lights the night sky so that one can see around themselves as if they were in the daylight, just as the Israelites did those forty years in the desert. This can and should be seen as a thousand years long day. The capital of the world in that coming age will be Jerusalem that will be bathed in *uninterrupted* light for a millennium. It gives added meaning to passages such as Isaiah 60:1-3:

"Arise, shine, for your light has come, and the glory of the LORD has risen upon you. For behold, darkness shall cover the earth, and thick darkness the peoples; but the LORD will arise upon you, and his glory will be seen upon you. *And nations shall come to your light, and kings to the brightness of your rising.*" (See also Isaiah 30:26)

Most teachers of scripture view this figuratively to mean spiritual light, though I maintain that the Bible often employs both figurative and literal language at the same time. Both Isaiah chapters 30 and 60 elaborate on this truth. Still not enough proof? Consider Jesus's teaching concerning the "last day." Jesus made it absolutely clear that the "last day" was the day of resurrection:

"And this is the will of him who sent me, that I should lose nothing of all that he has given me, but raise it up *on the last day*." (John 6:39)

"For this is the will of my Father, that everyone who looks on the Son and believes in him should have eternal life, and I will raise him up *on the last day*." (John 6:40)

"No one can come to me unless the Father who sent me draws him. And I will raise him up *on the last day*." (John 6:44)

"Whoever feeds on my flesh and drinks my blood has eternal life, and I will raise him up *on the last day*." (John 6:54)

When He said "raise him up" He was referring to all those the Father had given Him. This is the resurrection of the righteous dead! The fact that He mentions it four times in the 6th chapter of the book of John is in itself highly significant; God's word is telling us something very important here. The Bible speaks of only two resurrections separated by, guess what? A thousand years! This is found in Revelation 20:4-5:

"Then I saw thrones, and seated on them were those to whom the authority to judge was committed. Also I saw the souls of those who had been beheaded for the testimony of Jesus and for the word of God, and those who had not worshiped the beast or its image and had not received its mark on their foreheads or their hands. They came to life and reigned with Christ for a thousand years. The rest of the dead did not come to life until the thousand years were ended."

This is the Day of the Lord. A thousand years long day sandwiched between two resurrections, that of the righteous and the wicked. Jesus called it the last day and obviously taught it to His followers as evidenced by their use of the term. At Lazarus's resurrection, his sister Martha affirmed her belief that her brother would live again at the *last day* (John 11:24). Either the term was in common use in Jewish society (of which such an idiom doesn't to my knowledge seem to exist), or the master teacher coined it for His pupils. But the most telling proof that the *last day* is the millennium is when Jesus said that even those who reject Him will find their judgment at the *last day*:

"The one who rejects me and does not receive my words has a judge; the word that I have spoken will judge him **on the last day**." (John 12:48)

This judgment can only be at the second resurrection (known as the White Throne judgment) at the end of the thousand year day. Here we can see that Jesus recognized that the period between the two resurrections was a single thousand years long day, ***the last day***. The failure of mainstream Christian theology is in large part due to its failure to recognize the importance of this particular doctrine, the very cornerstone upon which its existence is built, the resurrection, both of the Christ and all God's elect. Without resurrection there is no Christian faith. Think of the big "E" on the Snellen eye chart; it will remind you of the Day of the Lord, the focal point of all ages. Let's recap this:

- The Hebraic definition for day is light that proceeds out of darkness.
- The Apostle Peter affirmed that the Day of the Lord is to be a thousand years long.
- Peter literally called it a *day age*.
- The prophet Isaiah told of a great light that would be over Jerusalem.
- Jesus taught that both resurrections will take place on *the last day*.

MOVING ON...

     Having established that the book of Revelation is about the ushering in of the Day of the Lord and that the form of the book was written as a narrative, let us proceed to make sense out of all its' components. Any story, regardless of the genre it represents, has a plot. The plot is where the action is found; the plot *is* the story. The plot of the Revelation moves toward the Day of the Lord; however, when it is read it creates a great deal of confusion. This confusion is due to the large number of small scenes found throughout it. It is much like watching a modern music video: The scenes change rapidly and often, leaving you lost even though the overall theme is not lost. God triumphs in the end. This muddled perception is aggravated by attempts to interpret it according to the form; you will never understand it through that approach. If however, you drop that mode and study the content then all will become clear.

     THE THIRD POINT THAT I MUST STRESS IS THAT THE ACTION (PLOT) IS FOUND IN THE SEALS, TRUMPETS, AND BOWLS. They comprise the bulk of the movement, the rest of the book being short subplots and character sketches. Remember my second point? The Day of the Lord is the subject (and climax) of the book. The seals, trumpets, and bowls lead up to that day. The content and form both find their climax in the 19th chapter.

NOW HERE'S THE SECRET REVEALED; THE SEALS, TRUMPETS, AND BOWLS HAPPEN **CONCURRENTLY**. Understanding this point will take you a long way toward deciphering the book. When the first seal is opened, the first trump is sounded and the first bowl is poured out. Then the second series followed by the third and so on until the seventh is reached. Notice the similarities between the trumpets and bowls:

"The first angel blew his trumpet, and there followed hail and fire, mixed with blood, and these were thrown upon the *earth*. And a third of the earth was burned up, and a third of the trees were burned up, and all green grass was burned up." (Revelation 8:7)

"So the first angel went and poured out his bowl on the *earth,* and harmful and painful sores came upon the people who bore the mark of the beast and worshiped its image" (Revelation 16:2)

"The second angel blew his trumpet, and something like a great mountain, burning with fire, was thrown into the *sea*, and a third of the sea became blood. A third of the living creatures in the sea died, and a third of the ships were destroyed." (Revelation 8:8, 9)

"The second angel poured out his bowl into the *sea*, and it became like the blood of a corpse, and every living thing died that was in the sea." (Revelation 16:3)

"The third angel blew his trumpet, and a great star fell from heaven, blazing like a torch, and it fell on a third of ***the rivers and on the springs of water***. The name of the star is Wormwood. A third of the waters became wormwood, and many people died from the water, because it had been made bitter." (Revelation 8:10, 11)

"The third angel poured out his bowl into *the rivers and the springs of water*, and they became blood." (Revelation 16:4)

The first series concern the earth, the second the sea, and the third the rivers and springs, etc. I purposely withheld the first through third seals because they do not *appear* to be similar to the others. I believe that this is because they are a bit more general, affecting the whole world whereas the others are more limited in scope. Think of a dart board [fig. 2]; it is divided up in concentric rings, each having a different value with the center, or bull's-eye, being the highest value. The outside ring would represent the world as a whole; this is what is affected by the opening of the seals. The next ring represents the trumpets which I believe are limited in area to a Middle Eastern theater. And finally the bull's-eye represents the dwelling of the Beast. The opening of the sixth seal, we shall shortly see, is what cements this teaching together.

There also appears to be a protocol to the plot; the last (bowls) is in time before the first (seals). This is apparent in the sixth of the series. Notice that starting in Revelation 16:12 the waters of the Euphrates River are dried up so that the kings of the east can cross over toward the west. This indicates a state of preparation has been achieved; the waters will act as a buffer until they are abated and the eastern rulers and their armies can proceed to the west. Lying spirits will proceed from the Beast, False Prophet, and Dragon and will go about influencing the kings of the earth to go to battle, and the kings will meet at

Armageddon. The popular concept that there will be a final battle there is patently false; all that the scriptures reveal is that the leaders, most notably those (Muslims?) from the east will gather there.

In Revelation 9:13-21 at the sounding of the sixth trumpet, we find the release of four angelic beings that were held at the Euphrates. These are doubtless the kings mentioned at the pouring of the sixth bowl as they have armies at their disposal. Whereas in chapter 16 they are static, waiting the drying of the river, in chapter 9 they are then released; in time sequence, 16 comes before 9. The bowls reveal the start of the action, the trumpets a continuation, but the seals show us the end result. Once again, I must state, the sixth seal is the one that cements this teaching together.

"When he opened the sixth seal, I looked, and behold, there was a great earthquake, and the sun became black as sackcloth, the full moon became like blood, and the stars of the sky fell to the earth as the fig tree sheds its winter fruit when shaken by a gale. The sky vanished like a scroll that is being rolled up, and every mountain and island was removed from its place. Then the kings of the earth and the great ones and the generals and the rich and the powerful, and everyone, slave and free, hid themselves in the caves and among the rocks of the mountains, calling to the mountains and rocks, "Fall on us and hide us from the face of him who is seated on the throne, and from the wrath of the Lamb, *for the great day of their wrath has come*, and who can stand?" (Rev. 6:12-17)

The events recorded at that time can be nothing else but the climax of the plot, the Day of the Lord arriving. Let's face it, if the things just stated were to happen this morning, then you won't be going to work as usual today. The signs in the sun, moon, and stars are exactly what Jesus said would immediately *follow* the Great Tribulation:

"Immediately ***after the tribulation*** of those days the sun will be darkened, and the moon will not give its light, and the stars will fall from heaven, and the powers of the heavens will be shaken. Then will appear in heaven the sign of the Son of Man, and then all the tribes of the earth will mourn, and they will see the Son of Man coming on the clouds of heaven with power and great glory." (Matt. 24:29, 30)

If we were to follow the form of the book, then we have a real problem; the climax has been reached at chapter 6 well before its time. It is an unfortunate fact that most expositors simply don't see that. This shouldn't be unless the events are scrambled out of order, of which they are. The majority of those reading the book get lost in it due to unclear thinking and lack of focus. Remember, we are interpreting it by its content, think of the big "E". THE SEALS, TRUMPETS, AND BOWLS ARE THREE DIFFERENT VIEWS OF THE SAME EVENTS. This fact shows us that there are actually only seven steps involved with ending this age with the Great Tribulation and the bringing in of God's kingdom upon the earth. They do not follow one another and overlap as some teach, but will happen concurrently. The climax to their action is the resurrection of the righteous dead and beginning of the Day of the Lord which is clearly seen as beginning at the opening of the sixth seal. The climax proper is actually seen at the seventh seal (Rev. 8:1-5), trumpet (Rev.11:15-19), and bowl (Rev. 16:17-21) as well as the whole of chapter 19. It is in the 19th chapter that the plot and content come together. It is, in all reality, a very simple concept when your focus is upon the one event, the Day of the Lord.

SO, THERE ARE ACTUALLY SEVEN STEPS LEADING UP TO THE DAY OF THE LORD. Upon the seventh step there are five things that will be seen on the earth: 1) peals of thunder, 2) sounds (voices), 3) lightning, 4) an earthquake, and 5) great hail. These are seen at the seventh seal (Rev. 8:5), trumpet (Rev. 11:19), and bowl (Rev. 16:18-21). They are yet another proof that the action is seen concurrently.

Now I know many of you who read this will have questions such as: What about the rapture? Who is the Antichrist? Or who are the Two Witnesses? The answer, depending on what you want to know, is that the Bible might not teach such things; they may be false manmade doctrines (as in the case of rapture), or they may be hidden identities not yet revealed. Allow the scriptures to speak for themselves rather than try to interpret them by your beliefs. Let the Bible dictate to you what is or isn't true. If you have true spiritual understanding, then you will have ears to hear what God is telling you. To sum up this section we find...

- The seals, trumpets, and bowls are three different views of the same events and make up the bulk of the book's action.
- The rest of the book is mostly made up of subplots and character sketches.
- There are only seven steps involved in ending this age and establishing His earthly kingdom.

- They culminate in the arriving of the Day of the Lord as also seen in the entire 19th chapter.

THE SEVEN STEPS

Now let us take a look at the seven steps. A good amount of Bible scholars hold that the number seven which keeps appearing in the Revelation indicates completion. The seven steps that complete this present age and begin the Day of the Lord are seen in three different views. I believe that each view starting with the seals becomes more defined and intense; the bowls or vials of wrath of chapter 16 being the swollen anger of the Almighty poured out on the Beast and his kingdom. Let's take a brief Boblical (a term coined by a friend of mine, as in "the Gospel according to Bob") look at the seven steps. To facilitate this process I designate the seals as the world view (WV), the trumpets as the Levant view (LV), and the bowls as the Assyrian view (AV).

STEP ONE

WV. Revelation 6:2 And I looked, and behold, a white horse! And its rider had a bow, and a crown was given to him, and he came out conquering, and to conquer.

The first step begins with a lightning military strike by the Antichrist, referred to in the Revelation as the Beast. The rider on the white horse is the man of sin himself which the world, especially those within his sphere of influence, will see as a great tactician and general. The white horse represents victory which the rider shall have in his conquest. This will happen at the mid-point of Daniel's seventieth week (Daniel 9:27). It is evident that this view is general in its scope; there is no mention of whom the rider is or is venturing out against. The scriptures do tell of a military movement in the last days when a king of the south shall push at the king of the north and provoke him to attack "as a whirlwind" with a great many chariots, horsemen, and ships (Daniel 11:40).

LV. Revelation 8:7 The first angel blew his trumpet, and there followed hail and fire, mixed with blood, and these were thrown upon the earth. And a third of the earth was burned up, and a third of the trees were burned up, and all green grass was burned up.

Beginning at this point it should be noticed that the plagues introduced at the trumpets are limited in scope. The first through the fourth soundings affect but a third of the earth. A quick glance at the 8th chapter affirms that they all fall within the same arena. It is my opinion that they will be limited to the area of the Middle East, the backyard of Islam.

At the sounding of the first trumpet a third of the world will be burned by hail and fire. It would be easy in these days to equate this to a nuclear cataclysm of some sort, which I readily admit is possible. Whether it comes as such or from a natural anomaly, such as a volcano or comet or even from a supernatural source, is to be seen when it happens. In the Islamic world, the Beast will be seen as the Muslim Messiah or Mahdi, first conquering and subduing other Islamic states then turning his wrath on Israel. One thing is for certain in my view; the plagues that originate here and in the rest of the steps are the direct result of the ministry of the Two Witnesses, as I will address in a later chapter.

AV. Revelation 16:2 So the first angel went and poured out his bowl on the earth, and harmful and painful sores came upon the people who bore the mark of the beast and worshiped its image.

Here we see the same plague but more intensified. It affects the earth (terra firma) and causes painful sores on the worshipers of the false Muslim Messiah who has just invaded Israel and desecrated the Holy Place. It should be noted that the Greek word for wrath used here in chapter 16 is THUMOS. Elsewhere in the book the word ORGEE is often employed, but in this instance it indicates a swelling, intense anger which is directed at the Beast and his followers.

STEP TWO

WV. Revelation 6:3, 4 When he opened the second seal, I heard the second living creature say, "Come!" And out came another horse, bright red. Its rider was permitted to take peace from the earth, so that people should slay one another, and he was given a great sword.

At this juncture, we can see the beginnings of a free-for-all fight. The rapid move to war by the Beast sets off a chain reaction throughout the rest of the world. It's like a cafeteria in a school when some kid yells "FOOD FIGHT" and everyone starts throwing their lunch. It is not likely, in my opinion, that his move to war is the direct cause for worldwide conflict (men don't need a cause to fight one another, it's in their sinful nature already), but it could be a catalyst. This verse does tell us that this judgment is sent from God as He controls the movement and the events that affect the nations. Regardless of what happens on the world scene, He is in charge and is calling the shots on the global billiard table.

LV. Revelation 8:8 The second angel blew his trumpet, and something like a great mountain, burning with fire, was thrown into the sea, and a third of the sea became blood.

This second step affects the sea in the Middle East. John describes a great mountain or something like it being thrown into the ocean resulting in the death of a third of the world's aquatic life. That this could be a meteor or comet is a distinct possibility. In recent years the topic of space debris crashing into the earth has worried many astronomers and other interested individuals. This is precisely what is believed to have happened on the 15th of February 2013 over Chelyabinsk, Russia. Upwards of 1,500 casualties occurred; mostly cuts and abrasions from blown out windows. It is believed by some scientists that it was an asteroid which came into the earth's atmosphere at a shallow angle breaking up into dust and many small pieces. The light alone from the flare was said to have been 30 times brighter than the sun causing some blistering and eye damage to unfortunate observers.

AV. Revelation 16:3 The second angel poured out his bowl into the sea, and it became like the blood of a corpse, and every living thing died that was in the sea.

It can clearly be seen that this exactly corresponds to the second trumpet sounding in chapter 8. It emphasizes that all ocean dwelling life in the Beast's domain is extinguished, where the second trump mentions only the water's poisoning. This is an intensifying of the plague and is directed at the Beast's kingdom.

STEP THREE

WV. Revelation 6:5, 6 When he opened the third seal, I heard the third living creature say, "Come!" And I looked, and behold, a black horse! And its rider had a pair of scales in his hand. And I heard what seemed to be a voice in the midst of the four living creatures, saying, "A quart of wheat for a denarius, and three quarts of barley for a denarius, and do not harm the oil and wine!"

Albert Einstein is credited to have said that, "An empty stomach is not a good political advisor." Truly, when faced with extreme hunger, people will make rash decisions in order to survive. At the time of this writing (February 2014) food shortages and undernourishment are a real and dangerous threat, especially to developing nations. According to the United Nations Food and Agricultural Organization (FAO) in the years 2010-2012, 870 million people were suffering from chronic undernourishment. That is 1 in 8 individuals living on the planet. In recent years, starting in 2008, a rise in rioting over food shortages has been seen globally and was a contributing factor in the "Arab Spring" of 2011 when millions of Arab youth began to overthrow their governments.

At the opening of the third seal, we see what appears to be a condition of extreme food shortage. The denarius, a silver coin of the first century, was considered a day's wage. With the war conditions induced at the first seal, the daily lot of millions could possibly be affected by hunger and poverty on a massive scale. This is already the case today. It is of interest to note that the crops singled out are the grains wheat and barley, some of the most consumed foods on earth. With these in short supply, millions could starve to death. However, it has been aptly pointed out by some expositors that this passage doesn't necessarily indicate a shortage of grains; it could just as easily be that the cost could be high due to the greed of those who control those commodities.

In recent years, although the bulk staple foods such as corn, wheat, and rice have been plentiful, prices have been at historic highs due to several factors. One effective stimulus is the deregulation in the commodities market allowing sellers to artificially jack up prices. This trend enriches a few individuals at the financial peril of the poor.

At this I would be remiss in omitting to mention the poisoning of our food supplies by the introduction of genetically modified organisms (GMO). All living things have a genetic code called DNA. It is in all aspects a written set of instructions composed of four amino acids which in certain sequence combine and form the chemical compounds that carry out the processes of life. These instructions are extremely complicated and no doubt point to a Designer for their existence. The combinations of amino acids caused by an interruption in the genetic chain could very well cause undesirable results and side effects not foreseen. This is especially possible due to man's dabbling in using DNA clips from totally unrelated species; a strain of wheat could potentially have a section of DNA from a water buffalo inserted. The use of animal genetic material in a plant chain should arouse the sensibilities of any straight thinking individual. Mankind is certainly not as smart as we think.

These genetically modified plants are seed bearing and have been released in nature often cross pollenating with natural strains. Genetically modified wild rapeseed from which canola oil is derived was found growing wild in North Dakota in 2010. Like a runaway semi-truck with no brakes they are now wreaking havoc with the food supplies of earth. At this point the monster has already been released to kill; there is no possible *human* way to stop this downward slide to destruction. If this sounds like a pretty bad scenario, it's because it is. Once again, man has assumed the role of playing God with the all too predictable results, like a grade B science fiction movie from the 1950's where a mad scientist crosses the line into God's domain. The destructive role that is to be played by these GMO's in the coming days of this age is now established.

In recent years large corporations have wreaked havoc on the environment and health of millions by the introduction of GMOs. Not only have they, through questionable business practices, bullied second and third world farmers to use their tainted seeds, but have sued some unassumimg farmers for patent infringement due to cross pollination, an act of nature. The official reasoning for their creation was to provide the world with high yield herbicide resistant food crops, a feat which has clearly not been accomplished. My personal thinking is that they were created in an attempt to patent nature for monetary gain. It is not my intention here to use this commentary as a bully pulpit against such organizations; there are plenty of individuals as well as activist organizations that are doing this currently. I simply want to illustrate the fact that man's greed and lack of love for his fellow man is hastening the demise of all people; this is a definite sign in this author's judgment that this is the last generation of this age.

LV. Revelation 8: 10, 11 The third angel blew his trumpet, and a great star fell from heaven, blazing like a torch, and it fell on a third of the rivers and on the springs of water. The name of the star is Wormwood. A third of the waters became wormwood, and many people died from the water, because it had been made bitter.

Worldwide, the price of food will have risen to an almost unobtainable level; the masses of people will be spending their waking hours with the task of feeding themselves and providing for their offspring. One third of the world as it was known during the first century will be horrendously affected by plagues, as seen in the sounding of the trumpets and the outpouring of the bowls. First, the land itself will be scorched, followed by the sea being contaminated, and during the third step fresh water supplies (lakes, rivers, springs) become tainted and deadly causing many deaths.

AV. Revelation 16: 4-6 The third angel poured out his bowl into the rivers and the springs of water, and they became blood. And I heard the angel in charge of the waters say, "Just are you, O Holy One, who is and who was, for you brought these judgments. For they have shed the blood of saints and prophets, and you have given them blood to drink. It is what they deserve!"

Once again, it can clearly be seen that the trumpets and the bowls mirror one another and thus illustrate that they are in fact two different perspectives of the same events. Here we see the waters mentioned above are now spoken of as blood.

The consumption of blood was forbidden by God from the earliest times of man's history, in the days immediately following the flood. The very being (literally soul) of a creature is found in its blood (Genesis 9:4) and the shedding of man's was to be accounted for. The people who are targeted with this plague are said to have "shed the blood of saints and prophets" and thus, as a punishment, were given blood to drink. That they should be labeled in such a manner and receive the punishment from God tells us that they aren't just an evil people, but are of an antichristian mindset; they reject Jesus as the true Messiah of God. These followers of the Beast are Muslims.

STEP FOUR

WV. Revelation 6:7, 8 When he opened the fourth seal, I heard the voice of the fourth living creature say, "Come!" And I looked, and behold, a pale horse! And its rider's name was Death, and Hades followed him. And they were given authority over a fourth of the earth, to kill with sword and with famine and with pestilence and by wild beasts of the earth.

Death is here personified as the rider of a pale horse. Hades (hell), also personified, accompanies him on his ride. This is an element of Hebrew poetry that few seem to grasp. Although the Revelation was written in Greek, it was the product of a Hebrew mind and culture. In the Hebrew scriptures, there is a writing practice considered to be a form of poetry whereby there is a seeming redundancy or repeating of an idea. This is most often done by stating the same thing a second time, but with slightly different words having the same meaning. A clear example of this can be seen in Psalm 119:105, "Your word is a lamp to my feet and a light to my path" where lamp and feet are paralleled to light and path. This type of writing is found throughout the Old Testament. In this passage, John parallels death and hades because they are the essentially the same thing, a concept echoed in the Old Testament (Psalm 6:5, 18:5, 49:14, 89:48, 116:3, Proverb 5:15, 7:27, Isaiah 28:15, 18, 38:18, Hosea 13:14, Habakkuk 2:5). How is this so?

The traditional "Christian" doctrine held by both Catholics and Protestants of an eternal fiery hell is a fabrication of Pagan origins; it is not supported by the scriptures at all if they are read in an honest and intelligent way. It is neither prudent nor necessary at this point to discuss the teaching; however, I have included in the appendix a short tutorial entitled *Hell*.

That Death is seen on the move here is only a logical result of the first three steps. We live in a global society to a certain extent, and what effects one corner of the world eventually will impact the rest of it. One quarter of the world, most likely the poorer, undeveloped nations, will suffer from war, famine or hunger, death and death by wild animals. This last is an interesting twist on the calamities that can and will befall mankind. We have an example from the Bible.

During the reign of Hoshea king of Israel, Shalmaneser V the Assyrian king came against him for failing to pay tribute and for seeking assistance from the king of Egypt (II Kings 17:2-5). He died during the three-year long siege of Samaria. His successor was Sargon II who finished the job by completely emptying the land of its inhabitants taking them as prisoners back to the cities of Assyria and Media (II Kings 17:6). After which, he brought people from Babylon and other ancient cities into the empty cities of Samaria in order to repopulate them. These people became the Samaritans found in the New Testament, half Israelite and half Babylonian who were much despised by the Jews. But, because they were pagans who did not revere the Lord, He sent lions among them to punish them (II Kings 17:26). The inclusion of this in the Biblical record is significant; apparently, a large number of the considerably reduced population were being attacked and killed, enough so that they petitioned the Assyrian king for assistance.

As the number of people grow on the earth the chances of deadly encounters with wild animals grows. A quick internet search will produce numerous reports of fatal attacks even by creatures not normally associated with them. In the last few years, many deer hunters across the United States, as well as other parts of the world, have been attacked, and some killed, by territorial bucks. Recently, near my rural community, there has been a deer attacking dogs in the yards of residents. Some of them have set up game cameras in hopes of identifying and dealing with it. As of this writing, there are an estimated two and a half million feral hogs, a large and potentially dangerous animal, in the state of Texas alone. In 2013, the economically depressed city of Detroit, Michigan, was inundated with packs of feral canines, as many as 50,000 stray dogs living in abandoned houses in dens of up to 20. They have caused interruption of mail service, as well injuries to humans and pets. Imagine what could happen in the wake of over a billion deaths: The void created in their rapid decline and absence, and the lack of food for animals as well as man.

LV. Revelation 8:12 The fourth angel blew his trumpet, and a third of the sun was struck, and a third of the moon, and a third of the stars, so that a third of their light might be darkened, and a third of the day might be kept from shining, and likewise a third of the night.

At this point, the light which comes from the sun is diminished by a third, so the moon does not reflect but a third of it. That the stars are affected tells us that the sun itself is not directly darkened, but the *light* from it is. The sun itself, of which its radiation heats the planet, if darkened by one third would plunge the earth into extreme cold and almost instantly extinguish all life. It is my opinion that what we will see at that time will be the result of man's interference with the physics of the earth. It sounds like science fiction, but there are sources that say some governments of the world, chiefly the United States, have the ability to alter the weather and direct its energy into true weapons of mass destruction. Once again, it is not my intention to express or explore any conspiracy theories; I am merely suggesting the possibility that such things could happen.

I do not believe that this particular plague will directly concern the entire world, but just the Middle East and Europe. This opinion is bolstered by the fact that the previous other plagues introduced by the trumpets are all limited geographically to a third part of the earth.

AV. Revelation 16:8, 9 The fourth angel poured out his bowl on the sun, and it was allowed to scorch people with fire. They were scorched by the fierce heat, and they cursed the name of God who had power over these plagues. They did not repent and give him glory.

The Beast and his followers are the direct recipients of the bowl plagues. We find here that the sun is the tool used against them. It appears that they will experience great heat so that men will be burnt while the surrounding area will, through anomalous weather conditions, see a reduction in the sun's light. At first glance, the conditions between the fourth trumpet and bowl seem entirely opposite of one another; yet, they both concern the sun. This selective punishment is in keeping with God's righteous judgment. He is more than capable of punishing the wicked and preserving the righteous in the same locality, as He did in Egypt during the ten plagues (Exodus 8:22-23, 9:4-7, 26, 10:23, 11:7).

THE FINAL THREE

Although there are seven distinct steps of God's judgment revealed in the book, they are not all of equal magnitude. The first four, while far reaching and terrible in their own right, pale in comparison to the last three. These are called the three woes, and the pain and destruction that accompany them will be epic.

STEP FIVE

WV. Revelation 6:9-11 When he opened the fifth seal, I saw under the altar the souls of those who had been slain for the word of God and for the witness they had borne. They cried out with a loud voice, "O Sovereign Lord, holy and true, how long before you will judge and avenge our blood on those who dwell on the earth?" Then they were each given a white robe and told to rest a little longer, until the number of their fellow servants and their brothers should be complete, who were to be killed as they themselves had been.

The opening of the fifth seal presents no action in the narrative; instead, we see a break. Up to this point the first four seals introduced some sort of action on the earth, but the fifth is a heavenly scene where the righteous souls of men are reassured of God's faithful justice. To the unenlightened reader, there are elements which can surely reinforce un-Biblical and pagan beliefs. The notion of an afterlife which many believe to be a Biblical truth *seems* to be supported here. However, this is simply not the case or import of the passage. Again, to facilitate the matter, I have added a small treatise in the appendix entitled *Concerning Death*.

It is often thought that the heavenly scenes in Revelation are actual, visible elements equivalent to things seen on earth (thrones, altars, temples etc.), that somehow men upon death could be transported there to see and experience them. Unfortunately, this is but a pipe dream. Jesus said that no man has ever ascended up into heaven, ever, except the Son of Man (John 3:13). This passage equates the souls of men with blood. There aren't millions of mankind's saved deposited at the base of a heavenly altar.

Under Israel's sacrificial system, the officiating priest when presenting in the sin offering the flesh of the animal sacrifice on the altar would pour out the blood at the altar's base (Leviticus 4:7, 18, 25, 30, 34; 5:9, 8:15, 9:9). During the second Temple period there was a channel originating from the corner horn of the altar in which the blood was poured down and which drained into the Kidron valley. Due to the fact that God sees that the soul of man is found in the blood (Genesis 9:4; Leviticus 17:11), we can detect the spiritual meaning of this text; those under the altar occupy the position of the blood offered in sacrifice. Spiritually speaking, the blood of the righteous cries out for vengeance just as righteous Abel's did (Genesis 4:1-12). These are not actual cognizant individuals literally crying out to the Lord for justice.

The importance of this passage is to introduce the reader to the concept of giving their life as a faithful servant and to foster perseverance in their faith. Concerning this time, Jesus was clear in His teaching that those who will endure to the end shall be saved (Matthew 24:13, Mark 13:13). Our lives are nothing apart from dedication and service to Him and His kingdom. It is all done for us, therefore it's up to us to receive His plan and enter into the kingdom.

LV. Revelation 9:1-11 And the fifth angel blew his trumpet, and I saw a star fallen from heaven to earth, and he was given the key to the shaft of the bottomless pit. He opened the shaft of the bottomless pit, and from the shaft rose smoke like the smoke of a great furnace, and the sun and the air were darkened with the smoke from the shaft. Then from the smoke came locusts on the earth, and they were given power like the power of scorpions of the earth. They were told not to harm the grass of the earth or any green plant or any tree, but only those people who do not have the seal of God on their foreheads. They were allowed to torment them for five months, but not to kill them, and their torment was like the torment of a scorpion when it stings someone. And in those days people will seek death and will not find it. They will long to die, but death will flee from them. In appearance the locusts were like horses prepared for battle: on their heads were what looked like crowns of gold; their faces were like human faces, their hair like women's hair, and their teeth like lions' teeth; they had breastplates like breastplates of iron, and the noise of their wings was like the noise of many chariots with horses rushing into battle. They have tails and stings like scorpions, and their power to hurt people for five months is in their tails. They have as king over them the angel of the bottomless pit. His name in Hebrew is Abaddon, and in Greek he is called Apollyon.

Now the trouble really begins. The entire world, but especially the region of the Middle East extending into Europe, Asia and Africa, will be inundated with a massive demonic presence at the emptying out of the bottomless pit. The bottomless pit is not a physical, tangible place, but rather it is a repository for spiritual beings, a jail or holding tank for the bad boys of the spiritual realm. These demons which are depicted as locusts are the exceptionally bad ones who are now being sequestered in order to protect mankind (1 Peter 3:19, 20; 2 Peter 2:4, 5; Jude 6). They are most likely some of the same ones who walked the earth in the early days before the flood and their release will be horrible for mankind. Quite a few translations render the Greek TARTARUS in 1 Peter 3:19 as hell, of which it isn't. The bottomless pit (Greek, ABYSSOS) and TARTARUS are, I believe, one and the same place or state.

This text relates that the sun and air will be darkened during their release. This tells us that the physical world will be affected. Their release is from the spiritual to the practical; the language is not just figurative. It is easy to see that the smoke itself which rises from the pit is actually the locusts in great numbers, but this is not the case. They are to come from out of the smoke. It is my opinion that when this particular plague ensues, the Lord will move certain nations to use a possible military strike by altering the weather and environment (most likely by Western powers) as a cover while releasing foul spirits to inflict pain and suffering on the followers of Islam, especially the supporters of the Mahdi.

Here again we see God's exclusive judgment on those who are to be recipients of His righteous indignation while His servants, who bear His protective seal, are spared the results (Revelation 7:3). The demonic denizens of the pit are not allowed to harm them. Some have sought to make this seal a special mark visible to all, but it's not likely or necessary that such a sign should be employed. The seal is the Spirit of God which He gives to all who receive His free gift of salvation (II Corinthians 1:22, Ephesians 1:13, 4:30). To put it directly, God's people will be present on the earth during the Great Tribulation, albeit protected from His wrath. There will be no escape via a rapture of the saints, which is a false manmade doctrine. I'm sure that this offends many evangelicals who believe in a rapture of the saints, but even a cursory look at history demonstrates that a large number of Christians were persecuted unto death in some of the most appalling ways. This fact alone begs the question: Why should the last generation before the kingdom age escape unscathed from the trials that have afflicted their brethren for almost two thousand years?

The angel over these released beings is named Abaddon, which translates as *destructor*. He is the one given the key to the abyss and has the special task of directing and controlling them. Their appearance on the earth and the role they play in tormenting men in the last days of the age has been foreordained by the Lord, and he will be their boss till the end.

Also worthy of note is the time period addressed. Twice in the above text it is mentioned that they will torment the unsealed inhabitants of the earth for a period of five months. This surely is not a singular or temporary phenomenon; the five months are the last five months of the age. The three woes that finish out the Lord's judgment are relatively quick in their fulfillment (at least, from an observers perspective). To those who will suffer this demonic assault, the time will certainly seem like an eternity.

AV. Revelation 16:10, 11 The fifth angel poured out his bowl on the throne of the beast, and its kingdom was plunged into darkness. People gnawed their tongues in anguish and cursed the God of heaven for their pain and sores. They did not repent of their deeds.

The Assyrian view is doubtless a concentrated and truncated account of the demonic invasion that the Middle East will sustain. The two basic elements of physical darkness and extreme pain indicate that the fifth trumpet call and the fifth bowl are two different views of the same occurrence, the difference being that this perspective is the center of the action. The Lord's wrath in its fierceness will be dumped out on the Mahdi and his militant followers.

STEP SIX

WV. Revelation 6:12-17 When he opened the sixth seal, I looked, and behold, there was a great earthquake, and the sun became black as sackcloth, the full moon became like blood, and the stars of the sky fell to the earth as the fig tree sheds its winter fruit when shaken by a gale. The sky vanished like a scroll that is being rolled up, and every mountain and island was removed from its place. Then the kings of the earth and the great ones and the generals and the rich and the powerful, and everyone, slave and free, hid themselves in the caves and among the rocks of the mountains, calling to the mountains and rocks, "Fall on us and hide us from the face of him who is seated on the throne, and from the wrath of the Lamb, for the great day of their wrath has come, and who can stand?"

For those who have a hard time accepting my view of Revelation here is the *smoking gun* of evidence to justify it. The pieces that interconnect at this juncture are numerous and convincing. In fact, I can't see any possible alternative interpretation in light of all this evidence. Briefly, I will direct your attention to five proofs that this and the immediately following seventh step are the actual climax of the Revelation.

Right out of the gate we're accosted with a great earthquake. This is not your everyday run-of-the-mill quake that the earth has known for thousands of years. This one is so intense and powerful as to move every mountain and island out of their respective positions (see 11:13; 16:18-20). This one is the one that many seismologists have designated as the "big one", the mother of all quakes. That is one bad Mama Jama shaker. A quake such as this will not allow mankind the luxury of going to work the next morning as if nothing has happened, business as usual. Such a quake will devastate civilization and would cause the governments of the world to collapse overnight, and rebuilding civilization's infrastructure would out of necessity take years, perhaps decades, to accomplish. This shaker and its results will be dealt with in a later chapter, but, suffice it to say, that its impact definitely points to the climax, the Day of the Lord.

Next in line is the clear effect upon the cosmic elements, specifically the sun, moon, and stars. Take a gander at what Jesus said concerning this singular event:

"Immediately after the tribulation of those days the sun will be darkened, and the moon will not give its light, and the stars will fall from heaven, and the powers of the heavens will be shaken. Then will appear in heaven the sign of the Son of Man, and then all the tribes of the earth will mourn, and they will see the Son of Man coming on the clouds of heaven with power and great glory. (Matthew 24:29, 30)

"But in those days, after that tribulation, the sun will be darkened, and the moon will not give its light, and the stars will be falling from heaven, and the powers in the heavens will be shaken. And then they will see the Son of Man coming in clouds with great power and glory. (Mark 13:24-26)

"And there will be signs in sun and moon and stars, and on the earth distress of nations in perplexity because of the roaring of the sea and the waves, people fainting with fear and with foreboding of what is coming on the world. For the powers of the heavens will be shaken. And then they will see the Son of Man coming in a cloud with power and great glory. Now when these things begin to take place, straighten up and raise your heads, because your redemption is drawing near." (Luke 21:25-28)

Not only did He forewarn of His return in power to the earth, He gave us an unmistakable time frame, *immediately after the Tribulation*! The same three cosmic bodies (the sun, moon, and stars) are mentioned in combination. They will be altered in a drastic fashion so that all men will see and experience the changes. This fact alone is undisputable proof that the climax has been reached, and it can only be through spiritual blindness that the majority of Bible expositors just don't connect the dots. The Mount Olive discourse cited above was Jesus' most revealing teaching concerning the termination of God's plan for this age. While a large portion is revealed through His parables, none are as direct and concise as that discourse.

As I stated previously, the quake that is to come will be like no other in intensity. The third proof is realized in its strength. Its shaking will be felt worldwide in that every mountain and island will be moved. This major seismic occurrence will cause so much death and destruction that a regrouping and reestablishment of society will take years. Even under the most favorable of conditions, such an undertaking would be very difficult, but after the events recorded in the preceding seals alone it would impossible on a practical scale. Life in this world as all mankind have known it will forever be changed.

Upon these things men from all walks of life, rich and poor, great and ignoble, will take to hiding underground in the rocks and caves in hopes of preserving their skin. This one fact alone speaks of the climax. The prophet Isaiah wrote about this specific time:

And people shall enter the caves of the rocks and the holes of the ground, from before the terror of the LORD, and from the splendor of his majesty, when he rises to terrify the earth. In that day mankind will cast away their idols of silver and their idols of gold, which they made for themselves to worship, to the moles and to the bats, to enter the caverns of the rocks and the clefts of the cliffs, from before the terror of the LORD, and from the splendor of his majesty, when he rises to terrify the earth. (Isaiah 2:19-21)

Lastly, it should be recognized that their overwhelming fear will be of the Almighty One and His agent, Jesus the Christ. It is obvious from the above passage that mankind will know that the Day of the Lord has definitely arrived and that His righteous anger is being expressed against them. Imagine the overpowering fear that people will have on that day that they will take their precious possessions and throw them at the subterranean animals out of sheer terror! Such behavior can only be due to total and undeniable desperation.

LV. Revelation 9:13-21 Then the sixth angel blew his trumpet, and I heard a voice from the four horns of the golden altar before God, saying to the sixth angel who had the trumpet, "Release the four angels who are bound at the great river Euphrates." So the four angels, who had been prepared for the hour, the day, the month, and the year, were released to kill a third of mankind. The number of mounted troops was twice ten thousand times ten thousand; I heard their number. And this is how I saw the horses in my vision and those who rode them: they wore breastplates the color of fire and of sapphire and of sulfur, and the heads of the horses were like lions' heads, and fire and smoke and sulfur came out of their mouths. By these three plagues a third of mankind was killed, by the fire and smoke and sulfur coming out of their mouths. For the power of the horses is in their mouths and in their tails, for their tails are like serpents with heads, and by means of them they wound. The rest of mankind, who were not killed by these plagues, did not repent of the works of their hands nor give up worshiping demons and idols of gold and silver and bronze and stone and wood, which cannot see or hear or walk, nor did they repent of their murders or their sorceries or their sexual immorality or their thefts.

Among the seemingly strange doctrines you may encounter in this writing, one that I espouse is that of territorial spirits. The concept is simple and logical, not to mention supported by scripture. When the Almighty One set His plan into action, He determined where and when the nations of the earth would settle. This He did for the purpose of bringing the elect into position of seeking Him out. Over the nations He placed angelic beings as guides, some good and some not so good. Their purpose and tenure is certainly not fully known and is subject to debate. What is known is that they do exist:

"When the Most High gave to the nations their inheritance, when he divided mankind, he fixed the borders of the peoples according to the number of the sons of God. But the LORD's portion is his people, Jacob his allotted heritage." (Deuteronomy 32:8, 9)

It should be noted that He predetermined that certain peoples would inhabit particular areas as is indicated by *inheritance*. Man is an organic creature, and apart from the physical world we are nothing. The earth is given to us as our lot, and He has divided it up to His satisfaction. The Apostle Paul addressed this very issue while on Mars Hill in Athens. Concerning the logistics of God's plan he said:

And he made from one man every nation of mankind to live on all the face of the earth, having determined allotted periods and the boundaries of their dwelling place, that they should seek God, in the hope that they might feel their way toward him and find him. Yet he is actually not far from each one of us, (Acts 17:26, 27)

He determined the times as well as the location of the nations which sprang from Adam. This He did so that man, being a free moral agent, would and could possibly search for Him, as it says that God does not want any to perish, but rather all come to His salvation call (II Peter 3:9).

The term *sons of God* is used in scripture to denote the angelic creation, and the passage in Deuteronomy 32:8, 9 doubtless refers to them. Their influence in the affairs of men is great, albeit not clearly known. I suspect that their role is to influence or "tempt" men to take action in matters of war and civil unrest, God placing them there for the benefit of man. Some, however, fail in their duties allowing sin and the wicked to prosper (see Psalms 58 & 82).

The four angels that are bound at the Euphrates River fall into this class. They are spiritual beings who influence four kings that have a large number of troops under their command. Exactly who these kings are and what nations they represent is a matter of conjecture. My best guess is that they will probably be nuclear capable countries with very large standing armies such as Pakistan, India, China, and N. Korea. The large scale devastation that they will incur appears to support this as does their number, literally two myriad myriad, translated as 200 million in some Bible versions. A myriad in Greek literally means ten thousand, although it's not entirely clear that the number should be so taken or if it is, in fact, representative of an indefinable or innumerable hoard.

AV. Revelation 16:12-16 "The sixth angel poured out his bowl on the great river Euphrates, and its water was dried up, to prepare the way for the kings from the east. And I saw, coming out of the mouth of the dragon and out of the mouth of the beast and out of the mouth of the false prophet, three unclean spirits like frogs. For they are demonic spirits, performing signs, who go abroad to the kings of the whole world, to assemble them for battle on the great day of God the Almighty. ("Behold, I am coming like a thief! Blessed is the one who stays awake, keeping his garments on, that he may not go about naked and be seen exposed!") And they assembled them at the place that in Hebrew is called Armageddon."

Once the Euphrates River dries up, the way will then be prepared for the four kings mentioned at the sixth trumpet call. Their unified presence at the eastern shore of the river raises many questions. Will they be preparing an assault against the Antichrist, or will they be there as a result of his call? There seems to be evidence that the former scenario may be the case. In the 11th chapter of the book of Daniel, we find the movement of the Beast in the last days:

"At the time of the end, the king of the south shall attack him, but the king of the north shall rush upon him like a whirlwind, with chariots and horsemen, and with many ships. And he shall come into countries and shall overflow and pass through. He shall come into the glorious land. And tens of thousands shall fall, but these shall be delivered out of his hand: Edom and Moab and the main part of the Ammonites. He shall stretch out his hand against the countries, and the land of Egypt shall not escape. He shall become ruler of the treasures of gold and of silver, and all the precious things of Egypt, and the Libyans and the Cushites shall follow in his train. But news from the east and the north shall alarm him, and he shall go out with great fury to destroy and devote many to destruction. And he shall pitch his palatial tents between the sea and the glorious holy mountain. Yet he shall come to his end, with none to help him." (Daniel 11:40-45)

There are at least a couple of things we can deduce from the above passage. First, the Antichrist is not a worldwide ruler as many mistakenly think. The king of the south will attack and provoke him to war. Second, the news that he receives from the east and the north will cause him to be alarmed, enough so to throw him into a do-or-die state of destruction. This may also indicate that the four kings assembled at the Euphrates River are there as a multinational force intending to come against him.

The end result of this *battle royal* is most likely a nuclear exchange that will of necessity involve all mankind. Revelation 9:17-19 describes what to modern observers can only be a nuclear exchange that causes the demise of one third of all human beings on earth. This coming tragedy will be Adolf Hitler and the Second World War magnified exponentially.

STEP SEVEN: THE CONCLUSION

The climax of God's anger finds itself at the seventh step. I've used the analogy of steps as in a staircase to bring home this point. As one would climb a stairway to reach another level, so is His plan with the seven steps to usher in a new level of existence for mankind, an idyllic world where nothing harms and the nations will have stopped their fighting. The night will be far spent and the dawn will be breaking shortly as YHVH through His Anointed One Jesus will make His appearance to trample the nations of the earth in His wrath.

A word is in order here about the period between the sixth and seventh steps. Technically speaking, the duration of the sixth lasts until the beginning of the seventh, but it will be noted that they appear to run together and overlap one another. These seeming discrepancies are not cause for concern. Their place in the narrative is secure and does not in any way detract from the system of interpretation that I teach or from the end result of God's judgment.

WV. Revelation 8:1-5   When the Lamb opened the seventh seal, there was silence in heaven for about half an hour. Then I saw the seven angels who stand before God, and seven trumpets were given to them. And another angel came and stood at the altar with a golden censer, and he was given much incense to offer with the prayers of all the saints on the golden altar before the throne, and the smoke of the incense, with the prayers of the saints, rose before God from the hand of the angel. Then the angel took the censer and filled it with fire from the altar and threw it on the earth, and there were peals of thunder, rumblings, flashes of lightning, and an earthquake.

The opening of the seventh seal and the establishment of the new level (the Day of the Lord) stand in complete opposition of the sixth seal. There the emphasis was on the mighty confluences *immediately after the tribulation,* but here it begins with a short respite of silence. I'm certain many have sought to read into and explain the meaning behind the inactivity and quietude in heaven, but the reason, while important, changes nothing to the point that the seals, trumpets, and bowls should be seen as anything but concurrent.

The appearance of the seven angels in verse 2 initially strengthens the idea that the trumpets chronologically follow on the heels of the seals, but I'm convinced that we have to forego a literal interpretation and see this as a literary tool meant to hide and obscure the meaning to those who don't have spiritual enlightenment (i.e. those who don't have *ears to hear)*. My observation is that almost always wherever we find the words *Then I saw* or *And then I saw,* etc., there is a change in the scene and we are introduced to a new element of the Revelation, often indicating either the start or finish of the Great Tribulation. Therefore, the introduction of the seven messengers here should not be understood as a continuation of the plot if we are to understand the book.

The introduction at verse three of the lone angel at the altar brings us back to the seventh seal. There he offers incense along with the prayers of God's elect. The incense is an allusion to prayer; as the smoke from it rises to fill the air making those present aware with a whiff of perfume, so the petitions of the faithful are noticed by the Father. The fire of the altar corresponds to the trials that generate the prayers. This fire is thus thrown back down against mankind on the earth and is literally seen as the great hail of the seventh step. The great hail is one of the five signs present at the final step: 1) peals of thunder, 2) sounds (voices), 3) lightning, 4) an earthquake, and 5) great hail. These are all seen at the seventh seal, trumpet and bowl.

This should drive home the point that the action here at the seventh seal is at the beginning of the last step. The affirmation of men that the Day of the Lord has begun was clearly seen at the opening of the sixth seal at the great earthquake, which is doubtless mentioned as falling during the seventh step, as noted above. In timing, the sixth seal will be at the end of the sixth step and the seventh at the beginning of the last step. There appears to be a slight overlap in the action between the last two woes as the writer states in 11:14 "The second woe has passed; behold, the third woe is soon to come."

LV. Revelation 11:15-19 "Then the seventh angel blew his trumpet, and there were loud voices in heaven, saying, "The kingdom of the world has become the kingdom of our Lord and of his Christ, and he shall reign forever and ever." And the twenty-four elders who sit on their thrones before God fell on their faces and worshiped God, saying, "We give thanks to you, Lord God Almighty, who is and who was, for you have taken your great power and begun to reign. The nations raged, but your wrath came, and the time for the dead to be judged, and for rewarding your servants, the prophets and saints, and those who fear your name, both small and great, and for destroying the destroyers of the earth." Then God's temple in heaven was opened, and the ark of his covenant was seen within his temple. There were flashes of lightning, rumblings, peals of thunder, an earthquake, and heavy hail".

The Great Tribulation is all but over. The Mystery of God (i.e. the coming of His kingdom upon the earth) has now arrived and the Day of the Lord is dawning. There is no other possible way of interpreting these events. To do so is to weaken the plan of the Almighty One and deny the truth of the gospel, which is the good news of His coming kingdom. The rewarding of the saints with eternal life and positions of authority within His new and all-encompassing government are directly tied to the resurrection from the state of death. As I've written before, the resurrection is the heart and soul of Christianity.

I often refer to His kingdom as new although there is nothing novel about it. His reign was established at the creation of both heavens (the spiritual as well as earthly realms), but the physical world was, through His plan, subjected to vanity in view of this day (Romans 8:20, 21). His plan is to bring together all things both heavenly and earthly under one head, His Anointed One, Jesus (Ephesians 1:9,10).

AV. Revelation 16:17-21 "The seventh angel poured out his bowl into the air, and a loud voice came out of the temple, from the throne, saying, "It is done!" And there were flashes of lightning, rumblings, peals of thunder, and a great earthquake such as there had never been since man was on the earth, so great was that earthquake. The great city was split into three parts, and the cities of the nations fell, and God remembered Babylon the great, to make her drain the cup of the wine of the fury of his wrath. And every island fled away, and no mountains were to be found. And great hailstones, about one hundred pounds each, fell from heaven on people; and they cursed God for the plague of the hail, because the plague was so severe".

It is obvious that the ground covered in this passage is exactly the same as that of the seventh trumpet. The emphasis here is not on the resurrection, but on the great earthquake that shakes the entire world. This quake is unique in its intensity (leveling mountains and moving islands) and in its timing falling within a pre-ordained hour. The judgment of the Mystery Babylon will take place and the city (not the literal Babylon) will be destroyed. I'll discuss this more during the look at chapters 17-18. Along with the earthquake, there will also be great hail of extreme size falling on the earth's inhabitants.

FOREST FOR THE TREES

If you have to this point understood what I have revealed, that the Revelation deals with the approaching Day of the Lord, then, believe it or not, you have actually conquered the book. You should have an understanding of its major points, that it concerns (1) the coming of God's kingdom upon the earth, (2) the resurrection of the righteous dead, and (3) the bringing in of the Day of the Lord. These major points should be seen as a whole, the climax. You should also understand that the seals, trumpets, and bowls are three different views of the same timeframe. Now you can observe and dissect the minor points that lead up to the climax, and which cause so much confusion for the average reader.

A terse overview of Revelation shows an introduction (chapter 1), followed by seven letters to congregations in Asia Minor (chapters 2, 3), then an overture (chapters 4, 5), and finally the plot which finds its climax beginning in chapter 19. A large portion of the book is made up of minor subplots and character sketches. As in any good story, the writer will develop the characters who take part in the action. The reader must have an idea of who they are and how they relate to one another, as well as how they fit into the plot.

I enumerate thirteen subplots within the plot. Within the subplots we find character sketches that inform us as to whom the main players will be in the coming days. Also found, and just as important, is the timeline for the book. As we look at these sketches and subplots we will see the recurring timeline of the Great Tribulation, 3 1/2 years. The following is my list of the thirteen subplots:

- The 144,000 and the great multitude Revelation 7:1-17
- Angel and the seven thunders Revelation 10
- Two Witnesses Revelation 11:1-14
- Woman and the Dragon Revelation 12
- Beast and False Prophet Revelation 13
- 144,000 revisited Revelation 14:1-5
- Three angels Revelation 14:7-11
- Two harvests Revelation 14:14-20
- A second overture Revelation 15
- The Beast and the Horns Revelation 17
- The Harlot's demise Revelation 18
- Marriage of the Lamb Revelation 19:1-10
- The return/climax Revelation 19:10-21

Chapter 20 is a record of the Day of the Lord; everything (content) before leads up to it. Chapters 21 & 22 are a vision of life after the Day of the Lord. It will be a period that will not be measured, as there will be no night. Although it is not the literary climax of the book, it is the end result of all the time ages, eternity as most understand it to be. While I presented the overview of Revelation by its content, I will approach the subplots and character development along the lines of the form, i.e., linearly from start to finish. Their meaning or significance is not in any way altered by this tactic; it is simply for convenience.

JOHN'S INTRODUCTION

John was a prisoner banished to an island called Patmos because of his faith. While there he was transported by the Spirit to the Day of the Lord where he saw the plan of God brought to fruition. Right out of the gate he indicates the subject of the book:

> "Behold, he is coming with the clouds, and every eye will see him, even those who pierced him and all tribes of the earth will wail on account of him. Even so. Amen." Revelation 1:7

The physical, bodily appearance of the Lord (Jehovah, Yahweh, or Yehoo as I believe His name should be pronounced) to the earth is the central feature of the Day of the Lord. Hey, you can't have a bigger headliner than God showing up for the show! In the 14th chapter of Zechariah we find this stated:

> "On that day his feet shall stand on the Mount of Olives that lies before Jerusalem on the east, and the Mount of Olives shall be split in two from east to west by a very wide valley, so that one half of the Mount shall move northward, and the other half southward. And you shall flee to the valley of my mountains, for the valley of the mountains shall reach to Azal. And you shall flee as you fled from the earthquake in the days of Uzziah king of Judah. Then the LORD my God will come, and all the holy ones with him." (Zechariah 14:4, 5)

Clearly God Himself is to make an appearance before the eyes of men. How is this possible? Does He have a body like us? Did He not say that no man can see His face and live (Exodus 33:20)? As God's agent in this world,

Jesus will on that day "stand in" for the Father and act on His behalf. This can only be accomplished in this way because the Father does not have a physical body as we do. Jesus made this clear when He stated that God is spirit (John 4:24). Such a concept is not novel; God used the model of agency many times in the Old Testament.

In the 3rd chapter of Exodus is recorded the story of when Moses was contacted by God in the burning bush. Throughout the whole encounter God Himself is said to address Moses in encouraging him to service, yet Stephen during his defense before the Sanhedrin distinctly said that it was an angel that appeared in the flaming bush (Acts 7:30). In Genesis chapter 18, God appeared to Abraham among three men (the number three isn't significant, there is no trinity) and announced that He was blessing him with a son. In Judges Chapter 6, Gideon was approached by the angel of the Lord, yet in the narrative is said also to be Him; the angel is used interchangeably with God. Agency is a viable way in which an indefinable and immortal being can move and work among physical mortal men. It works much in the same way as an ambassador who represents a ruler, the inferior "stands in" for the superior. The book of Hebrews sheds light on this subject by stating what God's messengers (angels) purpose is in His dealings with the physical world by ministering to the elect:

"And to which of the angels has he ever said, "Sit at my right hand until I make your enemies a footstool for your feet"? Are they not all ministering spirits sent out to serve for the sake of those who are to inherit salvation?" (Hebrews 1:13, 14)

All created beings whether they be men, angel, or animal are subject to the Almighty One and can by Him be used to carry out His bidding, even to speak and act in His stead. This explains why the Lord God can refer to Himself as "the alpha and the omega" in 1:8 and Jesus the Christ can call Himself the same in 22:13. Jesus, because of His willing sacrifice and sinless nature as a dutiful servant, gave His all and was exalted above all others to become the consummate agent of God (Philippians 2:5-10). Because of this He is worthy of our praise and worship. As Jesus told His disciples, "Whoever has seen me has seen the Father" (John 14:9).

John's first vision was that of Jesus standing among candlesticks holding seven stars in His hand. The vision is of course replete with symbolism, the seven candlesticks representing seven congregations in Asia Minor and the stars being angels or messengers that correspond to those churches (1:20). In Revelation 1:19, Jesus instructs John to write what is transpiring. Some expositors divide up the admonition into three steps; that which he'd already seen, that which is, and that which is to come, a seemingly cut and dried directive for interpreting the Revelation. These same instructors also tend to interpret the book by its form. This approach is convenient to a pre-tribulation, pre-millennial interpretation of the book and I disagree with this interpretation. The directive to write what he had seen was, grammatically speaking, in the aorist.

The Greek aorist is often and commonly translated as a past tense, which I believe is an oversimplification. The aorist is not a tense at all, having no reference to time. In fact, the name aorist means "without horizon" indicating its indefinable (as to time) character. What it does is indicate a completed action as opposed to the present tense which shows a continuous action or the imperfect tense that indicates past but incomplete action. In as far as verbs are concerned, the aorist establishes a fact. What the text tells us is that John is instructed to record the facts before him, both what he currently sees (the vision of Christ and the seven letters), and what shall come afterward (the Great Tribulation leading up to the Day of the Lord).

Among those who seriously study the scriptures, it is commonly believed that the number seven is allegorically used to indicate completion. Hence, we find in the Revelation the repetition of the number. Seven golden candlesticks, seven stars, and seven seals, trumpet calls and bowls being opened, sounded and poured out. Truly the number seven is important in the Bible. Its use in this first vision, I believe, underscores that the churches represented here are an overall picture of the state of the institution in this present age, not a pretty picture as He finds fault with the majority of congregations. Jesus, however did say that His church which was founded on a sure and solid foundation would not be overtaken by obscurity (Matthew 16:18).

An integral part of God's plan for mankind in this age that is largely and completely misunderstood is the nature of Christ's administrative organization, the church, the body of Christ. The church that Jesus began back on the shores of the lake of Galilee was a local group of followers of the one true God. What is its nature? Simply put it is a localized congregation of believers who have personally committed themselves unto God the Father and His Christ through repentance and faith. Having accepted the Father, and subsequently His plan of an eternal kingdom, the new believer then must submit unto the ritual of water immersion (baptism) and then take part in the work of Christ, preaching the gospel of the Kingdom for the redemption of mankind. The head of this institution is of course its founder, Christ, who by the Spirit of the Father directs those who willingly submit to Him. The size of the group is limited to a minimum of two.

Our English word church is a translation of the Greek EKKLESIA, a compound word derived from EK, a preposition meaning "out of the midst", and KALEO, meaning "to call", as in "to beckon." Together they indicate a called out assembly. We as God's children are called out of the world into His Kingdom and the church is the administrative body of its redemptive business. The origin of the word itself is shrouded in the darkness of Grecian antiquity. No one knows for certain who came up with the concept, as the recording of history did not develop until much later. What is known is that the ancient Athenians utilized it in the practice of democracy. All males who had at least two years of military service, regardless of social standing, were given a voice and vote in the affairs of the state. This definition is reflected in the Biblical assembly as well. Jesus taught that the affairs of His assembly should be controlled by those who served each other rather than through the domination that comes from a hierarchy (Matthew 20:26). In every case that it is mentioned in the New Testament, it always refers to a local, visible assembly.

The church as an institution is not universal. Two believers separated by miles and time zones are not members of the same church, yet Christ is the head of their respective congregations. If they each belong to a local group it is incumbent upon each to submit to the leading of Christ via the Holy Spirit yet only as localized bodies. They may both be members of God's family but not the same church. In this manner the church (in the institutional sense) conducts the business of the kingdom apart from any type of hierarchy. When speaking about it, I tend to use the term *church* hesitantly due to the widespread use of it to refer to its supposed universal nature.

THE SEVEN LETTERS

The purpose of this work is to provide the correct method and interpretation of the book of Revelation. It is not my intention to provide a verse by verse commentary of its content. There are many such works available to that end, some good, however a good deal, unfortunately, of dubious value to believers. John's correspondence to the Seven Churches in Asia Minor is often preached upon, taught from, or alluded to from pulpits around the world. I make no attempt to reinvent the wheel by attempting to draw moral lessons from them.

Among Evangelicals, of which I include myself, there is a popular and prevalent concept of the Seven Churches representing seven distinct church ages. I myself don't see it, but I cannot rule it completely out of the equation; such observations must out of necessity come from without the text itself, being fueled by historical accounts. I firmly believe that the Bible, upon close scrutiny, interprets itself perfectly. My view of the letters is much simpler; that they represent seven different types of congregations that exist at any given time throughout history, and Christ is admonishing or, when necessary, chastising them for their works. At any rate, their inclusion in the Revelation is important.

It would be a mistake to assume that the letters, while addressed to separate congregations, do not provide something to all believers in every church. The admonition to those "who have ears" is repeated in each one reinforcing the fact that the book, which is a letter itself, is intended for a much larger audience. The book of Revelation is indeed a letter written to seven distinct congregations, but is intended to be received by all believers for their edification.

A major point eluded to in the letters which I believe has major importance to understanding God's plan is seen in the mention of a group known as the Nicolaitans:

Yet this you have: you hate the works of the Nicolaitans, which I also hate. (Revelation 2:6)
So also you have some who hold the teaching of the Nicolaitans. (Revelation 2:15)

By name, this group is mentioned to the churches of Ephesus and Pergamum and, as is often in Biblical studies, subject to varying interpretations. Some hold that they were followers of one Nicolas of Antioch, one of the first seven Deacons in the Jerusalem Church who may have became apostate and began teaching false doctrine. This was attested to by some early Ante-Nicene writers of the second century, though not by Ignatius, possibly the earliest. Others postulate that they were early Gnostics who exhibited an antinomian doctrine (a setting aside of God's law=lawlessness) and a slide toward idolatry. The problem with such theories is that they, like the church age theory, are dependent primarily on outside sources or historical data. They are not mentioned *by name* as a group anywhere else in the scriptures.

Who are the Nicolaitans? And how are they important to the book of Revelation? That Jesus should mention them by name twice and pass judgment on their actions, I believe, is significant. They were a group of false doctrine purveyors that He said that He hated, a very strong statement declaring the mind of God. It is commonly held that the name is a compound derived from two Greek words, NIKE meaning to conquer and LAOS meaning people. Together they may express the idea of subduing or conquering over people. It is my observation that the consensus view among serious Bible scholars is that they were a specific historical group of heretical adherents to be feared and eschewed. My view is somewhat different. I myself do not trust the Ante-Nicene writers to be totally reliable sources of information. Although they were chronologically close to apostolic times, I see early signs of an emerging pagan influence in their written works. Furthermore, I am not alone in detecting an early Hellenization (adoption of the Grecian philosophical mindset) within the institution which Jesus began during His earthly ministry. It is my firm belief that the true faith delivered from the Apostles came under siege by evil men under Satan's influence even before they were all passed away.

It is therefore my contention that the Nicolaitans were not a specifically organized group under the leadership of a single man, but were instead a movement of pagan influences that gravitated toward a common goal, universalism. I am of the opinion that the Nicolaitans were the forerunners of Catholicism (from the Greek KATHOLIKOS meaning common or universal), a satanically inspired religious system having its roots firmly anchored in the ancient Babylon of post-flood days. Why am I attacking Catholicism? To answer that we must first arrive at a definition of it, then consider its implications and effects.

Catholicism is a natural and entirely human result and outgrowth of orthodoxy. Orthodoxy was a movement in the early days of church history that sought to weed out error among the congregations. Its name comes from the Greek ORTHODOXOS (from ORTHO = right, straight and DOXA = opinion, thinking) and together they mean "right thinking". Early in the second century, individual local congregations began to spread rapidly throughout the Roman Empire. These churches were all loosely associated having no central government. The earthly authority that oversaw them were the Apostles who played a big part in their founding. Over time, the Elders and Overseers charged with the task of teaching the congregants began to slip in their duties and, as a result of heretical influences, some congregations began to drift from the truth. This was cause for alarm to those adherents to the original faith. As is often the case with men, they began to take control of the situation by taking matters into their own hands by forming associations based on keeping to orthodoxy. As the influence of certain churches grew, some of these associations became more centralized and organized. Men began to form hierarchies, and some men began to subdue other congregations (the conquering of people, nicolaotism) as their power increased. Unfortunately, the orthodoxy became tainted in the process with pagan doctrines, most notably Greek philosophy. These were, I believe, the Nicolaitans whose deeds Jesus hated.

It is not as though Jesus during His life and ministry didn't realize the role such men would play in the days of His absence. He made it a point to warn His disciples and instruct them as to how to conduct the business of the kingdom when they were on their own (Matthew 18:15-20, 20:25). He was adamant that they were to serve one another and put each other before themselves. It is also an interesting aside to His ecclesiastical founding of the church to see that He did not leave explicit and detailed instructions for His Apostles as to how they were to organize subsequent congregations; He left the issue somewhat open.

The pagan influence and Hellenization of the churches along with the domination by men is the core of Catholicism. These Catholic churches have stayed in power and lorded over small individual congregations for centuries. This began early in the eastern part of the Empire, but in the western part of the Empire it was the church at Rome that gained the ascendency and became the standard for which Christianity is recognized (unfairly I might add) in the world. In the eyes of the secular world, Roman Catholicism is seen as the representative of Jesus' church. At the risk of sounding divisive or vindictive, I must stress that there is very little that is Christian about the Roman Catholic Church.

As to the pagan influence that defines Catholicism, I enumerate three: 1) Belief in more than one God, (polytheism), 2) belief in an afterlife, and 3) belief in an eternal punishment for the non-compliant. It can be seen through a study of world religions that these three core beliefs are recognized by most religions of the world, Islam and Judaism being the glaring exceptions due to their strict monotheism. I have aggravated many professing Christians by labeling them Catholic even though they were Baptist, Methodist, or Pentecostal because they held that those doctrines were true. In my view, if you believe these doctrines you are Catholic (universal), regardless of the label you place on your faith.

The majority of Christianity accepts the concept of a trinity Godhead which is incorrect and dishonoring to the one true God (Isaiah 42:8). It is no big secret that the one manifest distinction that the Hebrews had in their faith that set them apart from the gentile pagans was the belief in but one God. They held that YHVH was truly one individual as found in their creed, the shema:

"Hear, O Israel: The LORD our God, the LORD is one. You shall love the LORD your God with all your heart and with all your soul and with all your might. And these words that I command you today shall be on your heart. You shall teach them diligently to your children, and shall talk of them when you sit in your house, and when you walk by the way, and when you lie down, and when you rise. You shall bind them as a sign on your hand, and they shall be as frontlets between your eyes. You shall write them on the doorposts of your house and on your gates. (Deuteronomy 6:4-9)

If one were to simply read the Bible without the aid of a teacher or use of a commentary *and no preconceived notions,* it is doubtful that they would come away with any view other than that God is singular in nature. That fact is obvious in just the pronouns used of Him. In thousands of occurrences, the scriptures always refer to Him in singular pronouns indicating that He is, in fact, an individual.

The belief in an afterlife is born out of the desire to make man more than what he is, a biological entity. Mankind is distinguished from the angelic creation by virtue of his flesh:

"By the sweat of your face you shall eat bread, till you return to the ground, for out of it you were taken; *for you are dust, and to dust you shall return.*" (Genesis 3:9) (emphasis mine)

Dirt. It's really that of which we are composed, and as a product of dirt we are a tangible and mortal creation. All men die. We are subject to physical limitations and frailties from which the spiritual realm is exempted. Due to ambiguous doctrines and superstitious beliefs, men have fallen for a complicated scheme concerning the very nature of mankind. There is no clear scriptural support for the notion that man survives death either through his soul or spirit, much less that he "goes" to a spiritual realm such as heaven.

The ubiquitous belief in an everlasting punishment is a cruel joke on the uneducated and simple folk who live and die in this world it being clearly pagan in origin. The Hebrews of ancient times had no such conception of hell as an actual place of torment for errant souls. To them hell (Hebrew SHEOL) literally was the grave where all men were destined. Figuratively, it was the repository of men's souls. Understand that the soul of man is not a thing, but rather the state of being alive (see *Concerning Death*).

The tendency toward Catholicism began in the early days after the flood. Genesis chapter 11 tells how the people of the earth migrated as one people and collectively made the decision to deify and unify themselves in building a city and tower that was to reach up to heaven. That fiasco was thwarted by God and became known as the Tower of Babel. This I will address in a later chapter and is, I believe, the Babylon referred to in Revelation chapters 17-18.

One facet of the seven letters, which is exploited for doctrinal use, is the rewards for faithfulness cited for each church. Many expositors hold that there are specific rewards for those individuals who have kept the faith to be receive after death and use the letters as fodder for their arguments. It is my position that such thinking runs afoul of what the Bible supports. There is but one reward, that of eternal life. The rewards given to each church are nothing unique to them only; they are shared by all who are in Christ.

There is one other issue that I hold to be important, a clue as to how the book is to be understood. It is found in the letter to the sixth church, Philadelphia:

"I am coming soon." (Revelation 3:11)

That we find this statement from the Lord at the sixth letter, I believe, is on purpose. Remember that the physical coming of the Lord and the fulfillment of the Mystery of the Kingdom is at the seventh step. Starting at this place, we can see that He gives fair warning as to His return. We find a similar warning at Revelation 16:15:

"Behold, I am coming like a thief! Blessed is the one who stays awake, keeping his garments on, that he may not go about naked and be seen exposed!"

This is at the pouring of the sixth bowl of wrath. In this manner, Christ reveals to us, cryptically, that the climax to God's plan is soon to come about; it's just around the corner. As believers, we have the knowledge available to discern the nearness of His return.

- The letters address issues in those congregations that apply to all churches.
- A major theme presented in the letters is the danger imposed by the Nicolaitans.
- The Nicolaitans are best represented by the Catholic (universal) churches.
- The Roman Catholic Church is seen as the original representative of Christianity by the world.
- Christ warns of His imminent coming at the sixth letter.

THE OVERTURE

Chapters 4 and 5 are a preamble of sorts to the action (seals, trumpets, and bowls). In them, we see a picture of the heavenly realm where God, the Father, sits enthroned in glory surrounded by twenty four angelic elders (yes, they are angels), four seraphim, and before Him the manifestation of the seven fold Spirit. Jesus, portrayed as the slain Lamb of God, is seen as the only worthy agent to unleash His judgments upon mankind. The judgments are depicted as a scroll, sealed with seven seals. The allusion is clear: The scroll represents the SEVEN STEP PERIOD of Great Tribulation, the 3 1/2 years, and Jesus is the only one worthy and capable of opening them.

Chapter 4 begins with John seeing an open door into the heavenly realm. While observing the unobstructed entryway, he hears a voice like a trumpet beckoning him to come up to see what will take place in the future. Being immersed in the Spirit of God, he was instantly present before the throne of God and the heavenly hosts attending Him.

One interpretation of this passage used by many evangelicals makes this a representation of the rapture. The voice which sounds like a trumpet is seen as the last trump sounded to raise the dead and translate the living. It relies heavily on the three part division some erroneously make from the 1st chapter. They see the vision of chapter 1 as that which was seen, the letters of chapters 2 and 3 as that which was at John's time, followed by this introduction to the things that are to come. Regardless of the similarities in elements, this teaching just won't stand. The scriptures are clear that there are only two resurrections, that of the righteous and that of the wicked, separated by a thousand years. In order for this teaching to work, one has to ignore that fact or fabricate an alternative such as a specific resurrection of "church" saints as opposed to Old Testament saints. A secret resurrection of church age saints only is certainly without scriptural basis and is only born out of a fuzzy ambiguous theology.

It is clear at this point in Biblical revelation that Jesus is not the Father, who alone is God, but is His main agent in the world. This is evidently seen in His position *before* the throne – that seat is reserved for the Father only. Jesus is portrayed as a slain lamb which speaks of His obedience and submission toward the Father in becoming a sacrifice. It is He that oversees, directs, and carries out the work of redemption in this age, as well as meting out the coming judgments from the Father. The reference to His being slain from the world's foundation is in regard to His being in God's plan rather than to any pre-existent state. It was always in YHVH's plan that He would sacrifice His Anointed One in order to show mankind His willingness to receive them.

THE 144,000 AND THE GREAT MULTITUDE

In the 6th chapter is the opening of the first through sixth seals and the actual beginning of the movement of the story. Chapter 7 appears as an interlude in the plot, introducing two groups of people, the 144,000 from the tribes of Israel and a great multitude from all peoples. I won't get into a long discussion of who these groups are, but will be succinct: They are one and the same. Why do I say this?

The Bible is a Hebrew book. It was written, both Old and New Testaments, by Jews who had a specific culture and mode of expression. One such form of communication is known as parallelism, a kind of poetic way of emphasizing an idea by expressing it twice. By repeating the same thing in slightly different words, you stress its importance without being overtly redundant. It is my own belief (though I have no proof) that the practice itself was "hard wired" into mankind's brain and ordained by the Holy One for their benefit. John, the writer of the Revelation, was a Jew. He thought, spoke, and wrote as a Jew. It was his primary way of communicating. These two groups are the same, just expressed differently.

The chapter begins with a scene of four angels holding back the destruction of the Great Tribulation until God's servants are sealed and protected from the wrath He is to unleash. They are identified as the twelve tribes of Israel, God's elect people. This, taken literally, is what confuses the majority of Bible expositors. Most evangelicals, especially those of the dispensationalist school of thought, see God as having and dealing with two separate groups, Israel and the Church. I don't buy that. While I concede that He does deal in this present age with those two entities, they are very much mismatched. In His eyes there is not Jew and Gentile, but saved and unsaved. Either you are one of His elect through predestination or not. At the dawning of the Day of the Lord a remnant of Jews, those that are the chosen, will be saved and then all Israel will be redeemed to Him (Romans 11:1-26). If these then are not actual, literal Jews, then who are they?

You will notice that the 144,000 are seen *before* the wrath of God is begun. The great multitude seen starting in verse 9 is seen *after* the Great Tribulation. One is figurative (Israel) and the other literal. Here's why.

The Bible tells us that Jacob (Israel) had twelve sons. He also claimed the two sons of Joseph, Ephraim and Manasseh, as his own. At the time of the exodus of the children of Israel from Egypt, one tribe, Levi, was taken and given the priesthood service and was interspersed throughout the land of Canaan, having no properly defined area of their own. The tribe of Simeon also did not have an allotment of land; they were by prophecy scattered throughout Israel (Genesis 49:5-7). It is common among people to refer to Israel as the twelve tribes, though there were actually thirteen. This is because the sons of Joseph, Ephraim and Manasseh, being considered half tribes were thrown into the mix.

In Ezekiel chapters 40 to 48 is found various instructions for Israel that will be enacted during the Day of the Lord. The tribal list found in those chapters does not correspond to the John's list in Revelation chapter 7. Revelation's list consists of:

- Judah Reuben, Gad, Asher, Naphtali, Manasseh, Simeon, Levi, Issachar, Zebulun, Benjamin, and Joseph.

Ezekiel's list (chapter 48) is comprised of:

- Judah, Reuben, Gad, Asher, Naphtali, Manasseh, Simeon, Levi, Issachar, Zebulun, Benjamin, Dan, and Ephraim.

There is no doubt a evident discrepancy here. In John's list, Dan and Ephraim are not found. Additionally, Joseph is mentioned as a tribe, yet there is no tribe of Joseph. Surely John, a Hebrew, who was in all probability himself a priest[2], knew better? Of course he did! I believe this obvious mistake was written so that those with spiritual eyes may see beyond the literal and grasp the true meaning and import of the passage.

Although we are introduced to the 144,000 in the beginning verses of the 7th chapter, it is not until we get to the 14th chapter that we find a clearer definition of who these are. They are described as (1) having the Fathers name upon their foreheads, (2) been redeemed from the earth, (3) as being virgins, (4) following the Lamb wherever He goes, and (5) being firstfruits to God and the Lamb. Let's take a look at these attributes.

To be associated with the Father alone is a great honor indeed, so much more when one is positively identified as belonging to Him. The mark that is placed upon these is not a literal tattoo of sorts, but is meant to be understood as a spiritual identifier. Revelation 7:3 tells us that it is a seal that protects them from God's wrath. We also see that a similar promise is made to the faithful servants at the church of the Philadelphians:

"The one who conquers, I will make him a pillar in the temple of my God. Never shall he go out of it, and I will write on him the name of my God, and the name of the city of my God, the new Jerusalem, which comes down from my God out of heaven, and my own new name." (Revelation 3:12)

What is this seal if not that Holy Spirit that the Father gives to all His children (Ephesians 1:13, 4:30)? It is His Spirit that shields and protects us from His righteous indignation which is to be meted out on a wicked world (1 Thessalonians 5:9). To be sealed from His wrath is not something unique to the 144,000; it is a benefit to all who embrace the Father in repentance and faith.

If there is an argument to be found that the 144,000 represent a limited number of persons it could be seen in Revelation 14:3; those that were "redeemed from the earth". This could very well refer to those saints that will be martyred during the Great Tribulation and resurrected at the beginning of the Day of the Lord. The Greek word GEE (rendered earth) is used throughout the New Testament and can mean the earth proper (terra firma) or a defined territory, limited in size. At any rate, they are the ones going into that period. The number is doubtless a figurative sum (12 x 12), representing the fullness of His chosen ones and not literally the perfect count of those entering the fray.

That they are called virgins does not necessarily distinguish them from the rest of God's children. The Apostle Paul told the congregation at Corinth that it was his intention to present them as a pure virgin unto Christ (2 Corinthians 11:2). They are said to be *not defiled with women.* John is not indicating that this a literal group comprised of just sexually pure individuals, but that they are *spiritually* undefiled. The Biblical view is that women represented by our mother, Eve, who, being deceived, was caught in Satan's trap are subject to the same frailty (1Timothy 2:13, 14; 2 Corinthians 11:3). This passage tells us that the 144,000 are those who will persevere in the faith unto the coming of God's Kingdom upon the earth. All who take part in the first resurrection will share in this distinction.

The group is later found on Mt. Zion along with the Lamb (14:1). It is there that He will base the seat of His kingdom and they will never leave Him. The great multitude is also said to worship God in His temple day and night (Revelation 7:15), as also the faithful of the Philadelphian congregation (Revelation 3:12); this group therefore possesses no singular reward that any others won't possess. Jesus Himself taught that at that day there will be one shepherd and one fold (John 10:16).

Finally, they are called firstfruits unto God and the Lamb having been bought back from mankind. The use of the term firstfruits in the New Testament is almost always in conjunction with resurrection. Thus, believers have the firstfruits of the Spirit (Romans 8:23), and are themselves chosen as such (2 Thessalonians 2:13). In His resurrection, Christ is the firstfruits from the dead (1 Corinthians 15:20) and the predecessor of all who will follow. In all these points, the 144,000 do not differ from any other grouping of believers, but are in fact the same innumerable host found in the last half of chapter 7.

- The 144,000 and the great multitude are the same group.
- The period represented is the Great Tribulation.

ANGEL AND THE SEVEN THUNDERS

In chapter 10 we are introduced to an angel who comes down from heaven and stands astride the earth and sea. We are not told who this messenger is, just that he is described as mighty. It is his proclamation in verses 5-7 that is of importance:

"And the angel whom I saw standing on the sea and on the land raised his right hand to heaven and swore by him who lives forever and ever, who created heaven and what is in it, the earth and what is in it, and the sea and what is in it, that there would be no more delay, but that in the days of the trumpet call to be sounded by the seventh angel, the mystery of God would be fulfilled, just as he announced to his servants the prophets".

The clarity and simplicity of this passage is truly astounding. In effect, this passage tells us what the book of Revelation is about: THE USHERING IN OF GOD'S KINGDOM AND THE DAY OF THE LORD. For almost two millennia, the overwhelming majority of Bible expositors have glossed over the importance of these three little verses. To understand this concept is to understand God's plan with mankind. The 10th chapter is truly the key; it explains it all for those who have ears.

Not only does it speak of God's beautiful blueprint of salvation, it gives us a definite time frame when it will all come about, at the sounding of the seventh trumpet. This is what the Apostle Paul meant in 1 Corinthians 15:51, 52:

"Behold! I tell you a mystery. We shall not all sleep, but we shall all be changed, in a moment, in the twinkling of an eye, at the last trumpet. For the trumpet will sound, and the dead will be raised imperishable, and we shall be changed."

The last trump Paul makes reference to is found in the book of Revelation; it is the seventh trump. At its sounding the mystery of God is accomplished and the dead are resurrected. Blessed be the name!

"Then the seventh angel blew his trumpet, and there were loud voices in heaven, saying, "The kingdom of the world has become the kingdom of our Lord and of his Christ, and he shall reign forever and ever." And the twenty-four elders who sit on their thrones before God fell on their faces and worshiped God, saying, "We give thanks to you, Lord God Almighty, who is and who was, for you have taken your great power and begun to reign. The nations raged, but your wrath came, and the time for the dead to be judged, and for rewarding your servants, the prophets and saints, and those who fear your name, both small and great, and for destroying the destroyers of the earth." (Revelation 11:15-18)

At this point I would like to bring out an important argument. It is a common teaching among Christians of all sects that God has specific rewards for individuals when they get "up there." The concept of going to heaven is not a Biblical one. There is not a single verse that directly states that men, upon death, go to heaven. It is based upon a lie that started back in the Garden of Eden. The first lie told in the scriptures is the one Satan told our mother, Eve, that she would not die. She bought that line and men ever since have as well. It is indeed the origin of the doctrine of an afterlife.

As for the concept of rewards, it too is flawed as there is scant evidence that we will receive anything other than eternal life. What need or want could we possibly have for anything else? To have vibrant life, bodily, in the presence of the Father and his Son is all that we should want or desire. I have heard many sermons by well-meaning but mislead individuals about gaining "crowns" or attaining "mansions" in the "glory land." Some of those same men told of how they, upon seeing Jesus, will "cast their crowns at His feet." Wow! The Lord will be standing on a mountain of crowns! Jesus clearly taught His disciples that after we do the Father's will then we are to acknowledge that we just did our duty only (Luke 17:10) But, some may argue, did not Jesus teach us to seek heavenly riches?

To answer that question, we must first ask: Would our Lord use the sin of greed in the lives of God's children as an inducement to accept His salvation? Surely not! Would that not go against the clear teachings of scripture? Did He not condemn the Pharisees of His day for that very same trait (Matthew 23:25, Luke 11:39)? To appeal to the greed in man's human nature is like asking a bank robber to come and rob banks for the Lord. What then did He mean? The riches he spoke of weren't literal, tangible things; the heavenly realm isn't made that way. What He was prompting us to do was good works which make us more like the Father. To set our hands to doing good works is to have our hearts set on heavenly, spiritual things.

At the seventh trump, the dead are judged and the servants of God are rewarded with life. The judgment is coincident with resurrection which *is the reward of the saints* (Colossians 3:24). In summary:

- The Angel in chapter 10 sets the time for the resurrection, and the ushering in of the Day of the Lord (at the seventh trump).
- The reward of the saints is life at the resurrection.

THE TWO WITNESSES

The Two Witnesses of chapter 11 play a major role in the prophecy of the book. Their status and fame is near iconic, even though their individual identities are not revealed. I have been asked on numerous occasions who I thought the Two Witnesses of Revelation were, and every time it was by someone who thought they were the reincarnation of famous Bible characters. The return of men or women (either great or profane) in another body is a pagan concept and has no place in the theology of Christians. The Two Witnesses aren't Moses and Elijah, Moses and John the Baptist, or Moses and John Lennon come back to the earth to carry out some mission. They are two specific individuals who at some future time will possess the Spirit of God *in like manner* of Moses and Elijah. God will work through them just as He did those Biblical characters of renown. The acknowledgment of that fact doesn't mean that there are not some important things that we can glean from even a superficial study of them. There are, at least, a few important issues of note concerning them and their ministry. While their identities are as yet unknown, there certainly are some facts that we can deduce from the 11th chapter.

We find in Revelation 11:4 that they are positively identified as the *two olive trees and lampstands* standing before the Lord of the earth. This is an allusion to the 4th chapter of Zechariah where Joshua the Governor and Zerubabel the High Priest are cryptically called by that title.

They are called *anointed,* meaning that they have God's Spirit upon them (11:3). Because of this, I hold that they could possibly be representatives of the Israeli people, perhaps a political leader such as the Prime Minister and a religious leader such as the High Priest. I surely believe that it is possible that they can come from these backgrounds; however, it is clear that they will have to become followers of the Christ Jesus (11:8). Ethnically, they may be Israeli, but spiritually they will be children of the Faith.

Due to them being prophets, they have divine protection afforded them so that their enemies will meet death in a way proscribed by their words (11:5). This mode of attack that they will possess seems to have its precedence in the 1st chapter of the book of II Kings, where Elijah the Prophet called fire down from heaven to destroy armed men sent to take him prisoner. While the text does not state as much, it's quite possible that the men sent to retrieve him would have harmed him bodily once he was captured. King Ahaziah sent three detachments of fifty men with their captains to take him. Only after Elijah burned up the first two did the third captain humble himself before the prophet and plead for his life and that of his men.

One important fact about their ministry that should be clarified concerns their authority over coming events. They have the ability to bring plagues upon men and control the physical environment (11:6), which many mistakenly assume is in addition to those in the seals, trumpets, and bowls. This is simply not the case; *all the plagues brought about in the book will be directly due to their ministry*. This will result in the extreme hatred that those in that part of the world will experience toward them. It will be the viewpoint of the earth's inhabitants that they will be the cause of all their problems. Whether this takes place on a worldwide stage or a smaller regional one remains to be seen. The effects of their ministry will surely have global consequences.

As with the 144,000, the Two Witnesses' ministry sets the time frame for the book of Revelation, 3 ½ years, the Great Tribulation. This, it will be seen, is demonstrated in all the main character sketches; it is a recurring timespan. During the course of their preaching, they will cause all the plagues leading up to the seventh trump. After their testimony is complete near the end of the period of the sixth trump, they will be killed and resurrected. They will be revived at exactly the same time as all the saints, at the seventh trump.

The coincidence of their resurrection to that of the saints may seem to run afoul of the text; it appears that they are raised before the last trump. This is because the contents of the 10th and 11th chapters up to 11:13 are actually two subplots apart from the main action. In 9:13 the second of three woes began and in 11:14, where the narrative picks up again, we are informed of its end and the advent of the third. The great earthquake that will take place at the seventh step is clearly seen in 11:13.

- The Two Witnesses aren't famous Bible characters come back in another body.

- All plagues brought on the earth in the book of Revelation will be attributed to them.
- They will be raised at the same time as all of God's children, at the last trump.

THE WOMAN AND THE DRAGON

Chapter 12 is a subplot that introduces two important characters in the Revelation. The identity of one is ironclad (the Dragon is Satan), the other (the Woman) is moot. Like many other expositors, I once held that she was a representation of the nation of Israel. I do not now subscribe to that position. That she is an allusion to the nation is easy to understand. The elements in her description are obviously from Joseph's dream in Genesis 37: 9, 10:

"Then he dreamed another dream and told it to his brothers and said, "Behold, I have dreamed another dream. Behold, the sun, the moon, and eleven stars were bowing down to me." But when he told it to his father and to his brothers, his father rebuked him and said to him, "What is this dream that you have dreamed? Shall I and your mother and your brothers indeed come to bow ourselves to the ground before you?"

Here, the allusion is blatant. Jacob was quick to see the symbolism involved and chided his son. The sun and the moon are the parents, the stars his sibling brothers. Collectively, they are the seeds of the nation of Israel. That it is used in the Revelation is clear. The reader is supposed to think along the lines that she represents Israel, at least *on the surface*.

But we aren't interested in the obvious. We want to know what is behind the façade, the real meaning. That she is seen in heaven tells us, I believe, that she a spiritual representation of something. Let us consider the facts as presented: 1) She is seen in heaven, 2) she gave birth to the Messiah, 3) she will be persecuted by the Dragon, 4) She will be helped by the earth, and 5) the Dragon will pursue the rest of her seed.

No doubt this is figurative language. If she represents the nation of Israel, there is a definite problem with the identification. Revelation 12:14 informs us that she will escape from the presence of the Dragon. This just simply cannot apply to the nation as such because, speaking of that time, Zechariah 13:8, 9 indicates that two thirds of the people will perish with one third passing through a fiery trial. Yet the woman is said to escape and to be taken care of for the space of 3 1/2 years. To me, it becomes apparent that she is spoken of in language meant to make her look like the nation of Israel, but actually isn't. Who then does she represent and who is Israel?

Throughout the scriptures, we are reminded that Israel is God's chosen people. He called their father, Abraham, out of Ur of the Chaldees and sent him to a land that he was to possess through his children's children. They possessed that land, at least in part, and then lost it through disobedience to God's laws. Yet, they are still known as His chosen people. Are they in fact?

The short answer is no. Without going into a protracted discussion concerning the old and new covenants, I must point out that in God's word, the Bible, He reveals Himself to man on two distinct levels. One literal, concretely, and the other figurative, abstractly, just as when Jesus taught in parables. What I am getting at is that there are two groups that qualify to bear the name Israel: The literal one, a distinct ethnic people that have kept their identity for thousands of years, and a spiritual one made up of faithful believers of all nations. As for the spiritual people, Abraham is also our father by virtue of our faith. Paul taught that the children of faith are counted as the true offspring (Romans 9:8). The spiritual Israel is composed of both Jew and Gentile believers; to the Father there is no difference. Some dispensationalists have a hard time with the premise of all being one people. Many hold that there are two distinct groups with a similar but different inheritance, yet the scriptures are clear that a true Jew is one that is inwardly a keeper of God's law and not outwardly of the flesh (Romans 2:28, 29). It is my contention that the Woman represents God's elect, spiritual Israel. It would seem that a literal rendering would be necessary due to the mentioning of her giving birth to Christ, but this too can be easily explained.

In the 4th chapter of Galatians, Paul took an allegorical look at the very genesis of the nation, the two covenants, and how believers stand in relation to the nation:

"Tell me, you who desire to be under the law, do you not listen to the law? For it is written that Abraham had two sons, one by a slave woman and one by a free woman. But the son of the slave was born according to the flesh, while the son of the free woman was born through promise. Now this may be interpreted allegorically: these women are two covenants. One is from Mount Sinai, bearing children for slavery; she is Hagar. Now Hagar is Mount Sinai in Arabia; she corresponds to the present Jerusalem, for she is in slavery with her children. *But the Jerusalem above is free, and she is our mother."* (Galatians 4:21-26)

In Paul's day, the people (Jews) who inhabited Jerusalem were in spiritual bondage under the Law of Moses. Figuratively, it (the place of the Temple) corresponded to Mt. Sinai where the Law was given and codified, and Hagar who was Sarah's handmaid, a slave woman, to the Jews who kept the law for salvation. But God's true chosen ones have the heavenly New Jerusalem (Revelation 21:2) as their Mother. This is the city for which our father of faith, Abraham, anticipated (Hebrews 11:10). The Woman therefore represents the true chosen people of God, most notably those who are to inherit the heavenly New Jerusalem, of which also issued the Christ. He came out of the election.

This group of believers will, upon Satan being cast down to earth, be persecuted and pursued. They will doubtless heed the words of Jesus and flee that area when the signs of which He spoke become concrete (Matthew 24:15-21; Mark 13:14-19; Luke 21:20-22). Where they go exactly and who, if anyone, will help them is a matter for conjecture.

"And when the dragon saw that he had been thrown down to the earth, he pursued the woman who had given birth to the male child. But the woman was given the two wings of the great eagle so that she might fly from the serpent into the wilderness, to the place where she is to be nourished for a time, and times, and half a time. The serpent poured water like a river out of his mouth after the woman, to sweep her away with a flood. But the earth came to the help of the woman, and the earth opened its mouth and swallowed the river that the dragon had poured from his mouth". (Revelation 12:13-16)

There are two things I would like to point out in the above verses: 1) The use of the word *earth,* and 2) the use of the Greek middle voice in places. First, the word translated earth (GHEE) is in exact meaning the physical earth. Satan will be cast down, out of heaven, onto the land itself; that spiritual being will be relegated to the physical plane.

This tells us that he is an actual being and not just a figurative representation of evil, as some believe and teach. No longer will he be able to dwell in the heavenly realm, but will be consigned to an earthly dimension. The land itself will act as a physical buffer between those who have fled and their pursuers. Water is used allegorically in scripture for people (Revelation 17:15) and it may be that the stream that issues from the Dragon could be assassins or armies sent out and swallowed up by the land.

In English grammar, there are two voices. Active, where the subject does the action (*Bob robbed the bank.*), and passive, where the subject receives the action (*The bank robbed Bob.*) However, in Greek there is another type of voice known as the middle, a cross between the others where the subject does the action but receives the benefit thereof (*Bob robbed the bank for himself.*) There is no equivalent in English. This is employed where the Woman flies (for herself) and is nourished (feeds herself), giving the impression that perhaps it's a self-protective action. One prevalent idea that dispensationalists espouse is that the Woman is literal Israel, and that she will be air lifted out by the U.S. Air force and protected by her invincible ally, America (yeah right). Hey, anything's possible, but I don't necessarily foresee it happening.

After the Woman makes her escape, the Dragon will wage a war of extermination on her remaining children. These will be those elect who are to obtain salvation. These poor saints will be left in the Levant and the regional Islamic countries to suffer at the hands of Muslim fanatics, who will be key players in the Great Tribulation. What makes me think this? In Revelation 20:4 John saw the resurrected people who had been *beheaded* by the Antichrist for the cause of Christ. In this current world, only one major religion practices that cruel form of punishment: Islam.

It should also be noted that the Dragon, Satan, is represented as having seven heads and ten horns, a description he shares with the Beast of the next chapter. While I will address the symbolism in their appearance in a coming chapter, suffice it to say that it is political in nature. Satan, who is the god of this world (2 Corinthians 4:4) and the prince of the power of the air (Ephesians 2:2), works within the governments of earth to accomplish his end.

As with the Two Witnesses, the timeframe for this subplot is 3 ½ years. Let's recap this:

- The Woman represents God's elect.
- They will be granted to escape from the Dragon's wrath.

- After the vigilant elect make their escape, Satan will move fanatical Islamists to exterminate the remaining saints.

THE BEAST AND THE FALSE PROPHET

The 13th chapter of Revelation is, along with the 17th chapter, the most revealing, and yet, I think, the most misunderstood part of eschatology. They go hand in hand; 17 explains 13. Yet, those who consider its detail often jump to conclusions with scant proof to back up their presumptions. I've pondered its content for years without committing to any definite interpretation. There are now, I believe, some facts which can be established and used to ascertain the identity and role of the Antichrist when his time comes at the end of this age.

First off, at the time of this writing, I haven't the slightest idea as to the exact identities of the Antichrist or his False Prophet. The proclivity of some expositors to positively name them is unwise and unproductive to the task of understanding the book as a whole. There are obviously enough details revealed that when the time comes they will be clearly recognized. This much I am willing to commit to; however, the Antichrist is not the Pope, Prince Charles of England, or Jack the Ripper reincarnated.

To begin, it is best to reference the 13th chapter of Revelation. It is there that the reader is formally introduced to the Beast and his cohort, the False Prophet:

"And I saw a beast rising out of the sea, with ten horns and seven heads, with ten diadems on its horns and blasphemous names on its heads. And the beast that I saw was like a leopard; its feet were like a bear's, and its mouth was like a lion's mouth. And to it the dragon gave his power and his throne and great authority. One of its heads seemed to have a mortal wound, but its mortal wound was healed, and the whole earth marveled as they followed the beast. And they worshiped the dragon, for he had given his authority to the beast, and they worshiped the beast, saying, "Who is like the beast, and who can fight against it?" And the beast was given a mouth uttering haughty and blasphemous words, and it was allowed to exercise authority for forty-two months." (Revelation 13:1-5)

In the previous chapter, we saw mankind's adversary, Satan, described as a Dragon having seven heads and ten horns. Here, we are now introduced to a separate creature called in the Greek a THERION (a wild or venomous beast), and it too shares the same exact description, seven heads and ten horns. In addition, John saw that it appeared as an amalgamation of a lion, bear, and leopard. The same animals that Daniel described as the kingdoms of Babylon, Persia, and Greece (Daniel 7:4-6). At the outset, we must bear in mind that even though they share the same basic description, they are two distinct entities working through the same system.

The reason that both Satan and the Antichrist share the same features is because the features represent the same thing, human government. We have the key to this truth in Revelation 17:8-13:

"The beast that you saw was, and is not, and is about to rise from the bottomless pit and go to destruction. And the dwellers on earth whose names have not been written in the book of life from the foundation of the world will marvel to see the beast, because it was and is not and is to come. This calls for a mind with wisdom: the seven heads are seven mountains on which the woman is seated; they are also seven kings, five of whom have fallen, one is, the other has not yet come, and when he does come he must remain only a little while. As for the beast that was and is not, it is an eighth but it belongs to the seven, and it goes to destruction. And the ten horns that you saw are ten kings who have not yet received royal power, but they are to receive authority as kings for one hour, together with the beast. These are of one mind, and they hand over their power and authority to the beast."

The Beast's heads represent seven mountains. At this point, many teachers lose the trail by viewing the mountains as an actual geological feature. One prevalent teaching among Protestants is that the Beast is the Roman Catholic Church due to Rome being known as the city of seven hills. But, mountain as used in this context is representative of a kingdom, for they also represent seven kings. There is Biblical precedence for this interpretation found in the book of Daniel. In its 2nd chapter, we find the story of Nebuchadnezzar's dream, where he saw a great statue made of different minerals, each inferior in value to the one preceding it, beginning at the head and going down to the feet. This great statue was destroyed by a cut stone that was made without human hands when it was struck on its feet. The cut stone then became a mountain that filled the whole earth. The statue represented kingdoms that were conquered by an individual, Christ, seen as the stone who will then become the king of a worldwide kingdom, the millennial kingdom. The mountain is allegorical language for a kingdom.

The seven heads are thus seven kingdoms, as well as seven individual kings. It is my position that the seven were appointed specifically by God to each play a part in His overall plan for the ages. The Antichrist is an eighth ruler who once was active in one of the other seven kingdoms. How can this be? Is he a reincarnated person? In short answer, no. The king that will rise from the abyss is actually an angelic being, a demon, which was once active in influencing human government in one of those kingdoms. This is referred to as a territorial spirit by some theologians. It is commonly thought that the Antichrist will be a man that will be assassinated and then come back to life, but that view is flawed and is based on unclear thinking. The head that was wounded is an angelic being (territorial spirit) that will be allowed to come out of the spiritual prison (11:7), where he, as well as others, are now being sequestered (Revelation 9:2-4).

The seven heads are kingdoms that were spiritually influenced and affected God's elect. Five of them had in John's day already fallen; one was in power then, and one was yet to come and last but a short while. To my thinking, the five that had already fallen were Egypt, Assyria, Babylon, Media-Persia, and Greece. The one that existed at the writing of the Revelation was Rome, and the one that was yet to come and endure for a short period was Nazi Germany, the Third Reich. Each of these human governments was, in my opinion, influenced by spiritual beings.

Although the Beast itself is an allegorical representation of certain human governments, the Antichrist is called by that moniker as well. Starting at 13:3, the emphasis shifts from the kingdom to the ruler. I personally believe this is because he will be the embodiment of all the spiritual evil directed against God's elect in the Islamic countries. This ruler is the one seen at the opening of the first seal, the bow carrying conqueror on the white horse. His military prowess will earn him the admiration and worship of the people associated with him, the Muslims. He will be worshiped as the Mahdi, the Islamic Messiah that will come to conquer the world and set things right.

Perhaps now many of you are wondering why I am pointing the finger at Islam. I fully realize that for many I must seem to be divisive or closed minded, but the Biblical support for my doctrine is sufficient proof for me to take the position that I do. A proper understanding of what makes the Antichrist what he is will go a long way in determining Islam's role in the Revelation. Also, in order to understand the Revelation, the Prophets (including the book of Daniel) must be examined. It covers much of the same eschatological ground, both literally and allegorically.

"Children, it is the last hour, and as you have heard that antichrist is coming, so now many antichrists have come. Therefore we know that it is the last hour. They went out from us, but they were not of us; for if they had been of us, they would have continued with us. But they went out, that it might become plain that they all are not of us. But you have been anointed by the Holy One, and you all have knowledge. I write to you, not because you do not know the truth, but because you know it, and because no lie is of the truth. Who is the liar but he who denies that Jesus is the Christ? This is the antichrist, he who denies the Father and the Son." (1 John 2:18-22)

"By this you know the Spirit of God: every spirit that confesses that Jesus Christ has come in the flesh is from God, and every spirit that does not confess Jesus is not from God. This is the spirit of the antichrist, which you heard was coming and now is in the world already." (1 John 4:2-3)

Straight from the gate the Apostle John tells us what quality for which the Antichrist will be known: He will deny that Jesus was the actual Messiah come in the flesh. The title Messiah means *anointed*. He is one who is set aside to perform a specific task, to set all things aright in this world. Even the Samaritans, which were a Semitic people who adopted the Mosaic Law in part, looked to His arrival. In the 4th chapter of the gospel of John, the Samaritan woman at the well told Jesus that she knew that when the Messiah comes that He would explain all things (John 4:25), most likely a belief held by those of her people. Even to the average Christian, this truth is scant understood. Here in the Western hemisphere, there are many that actually think that the title *Christ*, the Greek term for anointed, is Jesus' last name. The Messiah of God is a singular phenomenon. True, there are many anointed, but there is only one who is *the* Anointed, the consummate agent of the Almighty, and this is Jesus. Due to the prevailing spirit, John was clear that there were many antichrists even in his day, but the man of sin was yet to appear.

Any faith that denies that Jesus is the true Messiah come from the Father can therefore be in the spirit of antichrist (Judaism, Islam, Hinduism, Christianity, et al.). What convinces me that Islam is the culprit is its prevalence in world affairs in the Middle East. Islam clearly denies that

Jesus is the anointed of God, claiming that the Mahdi will come to set all things right with Issa (Jesus) accompanying him to perform wondrous miracles. This Issa will be the Antichrist's False Prophet. The Mahdi will be an obnoxious fellow, a blasphemer of the highest order, who will verbally attack the Almighty One in a spiritual battle. His method will be to curse His name, His dwelling, and His heavenly support:

"And he opened his mouth for blasphemies against God, to blaspheme his name, and his tabernacle, *even* them that dwell in the heaven." (Revelation 13:6 ASV)

Name in the scriptures is often used to indicate authority. The one bearing about the name of a person is the agent of that person, and therefore speaks and acts in their behalf and/or absence. It is certain that the Beast will deny God's authority in any and all matters, but not just a generic god whom most people recognize, but the one true God whose people are named after Him. The accepted majority view among adherents of Christianity is that God is seen in an impersonal manner as a "substance" of three distinct beings, i.e. a Trinity. This is not the case among the other faiths of the world that worship distinct gods bearing specific names. However, there are today more professing Christians who speak of the Almighty One by His personal name, the pronunciation of which is not universally agreed upon. Some groups call Him Jehovah, others Yahweh, and still others by variants based upon their Hebraic research. The Hebrew letters for His name are yud, hey, vav, hey (English equivalent YHVH). My personal belief is that it should be pronounced Yehoo (phonetically spelled) based on the Hebraic pronunciation of Judah, Yehudah (yeh hoo dah), with the dalet (D) dropped. The name Judah (YHVDH), which means *I will praise YHVH,* is almost identical with the tetragram YHVH. Regardless of one's preference, I believe that the name of God will once again be uttered by the High Priest of Israel in the coming days.

The Tabernacle of YHVH presents an interpretive problem. The Greek word SKENE used in this passage literally refers to a tent, but is often translated figuratively as dwelling. This may be due to the Hebrew word used for tabernacle in the Old Testament, MISHKAN, which comes from the root meaning to sit or dwell. The Tabernacle of YHVH hosted the visible dwelling of Him on earth. Taken figuratively, it could be a reference to the spiritual dwelling, heaven, wherein the Almighty One resides. The Tabernacle was a shadow or type of His dwelling based upon a spiritual reality.

There is, however, in my way of thinking, another possible way this can be interpreted. It could be that the passage should be taken literally. The Tabernacle is the actual tent that was made by the children of Israel as directed by YHVH. It was at its best a temporary resting place, so to speak, of the Immortal Spirit; a tent is a mobile habitation. While it may sound fantastic, I believe that there is a very good chance that the actual artifact may be found soon along with its furnishings, including the Ark of the Covenant. The implications of such a find for Biblical prophecy are many and astounding. It's a real game changer. This I will discuss in the next chapter.

The Beast will talk against those spiritual beings who attend the Almighty One. He is a man possessed by a spiritual being who will then be back in commission in the spiritual warfare that exists in the heavenly realm (Ephesians 6:12). Which king(s) he inhabited (possessed) in the past is a matter for conjecture. I am of the opinion that he inhabited the Seleucid ruler Antiochus Epiphanies, who, it can be argued, was certainly a type of the Antichrist to come. It was he who profaned the second Temple by offering swine on its altar to the god Jupiter. The Beast is the Antichrist and is also called *the man of sin* (lawlessness) and *the son of perdition* (destruction), (2 Thessalonians 2:3).

His assistant, the miracle working False Prophet, Issa, will establish a system (vs. 16-18) whereby no person will be able to transact business for any reason without a mark upon their forehead or right hand. The mark will be either the name or number of the Beast, which is described as the number of a man, 666.

Much has been written concerning his infamous identity. I myself am not skilled in the art of Hebrew gematria, having not the wisdom to count and calculate his name and number. However, this much I will say concerning the efforts of many others: Calculating numbers derived from English names or other alphabets is at best questionable, if not unwise. The safe thing to do, at least in my case, is to not attempt to fit some individual, profane or otherwise, into a mold on the strength of a misunderstood science. Perhaps somewhere today, there is someone who has that wisdom and knows the identity, but I surely do not.

It would certainly be a fatal mistake, doctrinally speaking, to ignore the Hebrew Prophets who wrote concerning the last days of this age. The Beast plays such a pivotal role in the coming days that he must surely have been spoken about by them, and indeed he was. His ethnic identity and political associations were revealed openly by the Prophets Isaiah, Ezekiel and Daniel with references in Micah, Zephaniah and Nahum, and yet he is hidden in plain sight. He is spoken of in a way that makes me think that the reader would or should be familiar with him, and, indeed, we are to be. There are several designations ascribed to the coming Antichrist in the prophetical books. He is called by the titles of prince, the king of Assyria and the king of Babylon, and by name, Gog.

The best place to go to get a handle on the Antichrist's ethnicity is 10th chapter of Isaiah. The prophecies of Isaiah are largely about him and the following Day of the Lord. Beginning at 10:4, we find the Assyrian introduced as the rod of YHVH's anger who trods over nations and conquers without realizing he is a puppet of YHVH. He is a megalomanical tyrant who thinks he is in control of all the goings on in his part of the world, but the Lord is the one who's pulling the strings:

Ah, Assyria, the rod of my anger; the staff in their hands is my fury! Against a godless nation I send *him*, and against the people of my wrath I command *him*, to take spoil and seize plunder, and to tread them down like the mire of the streets. But *he* does not so intend, and *his* heart does not so think; but it is in *his* heart to destroy, and to cut off nations not a few; (Isaiah 10:5-7 *italics* mine)

In the wake of his path of destruction, nations will be left destitute their ruin, a testament to his ferocious nature. He will be the envy of those disposed to his faith, who will exclaim "Who is like the beast, and who can fight against it?" (Revelation 13:4). Yet, in his overwhelming power and military prowess, he also will suffer the judgment of the Almighty One:

> "When the Lord has finished all his work on Mount Zion and on Jerusalem, he will punish the speech of the arrogant heart of the king of Assyria and the boastful look in his eyes. For he says: "By the strength of my hand I have done it, and by my wisdom, for I have understanding; I remove the boundaries of peoples, and plunder their treasures; like a bull I bring down those who sit on thrones. My hand has found like a nest the wealth of the peoples; and as one gathers eggs that have been forsaken, so I have gathered all the earth; and there was none that moved a wing or opened the mouth or chirped." Shall the axe boast over him who hews with it, or the saw magnify itself against him who wields it? As if a rod should wield him who lifts it, or as if a staff should lift him who is not wood! Therefore the Lord GOD of hosts will send wasting sickness among his stout warriors, and under his glory a burning will be kindled, like the burning of fire. The light of Israel will become a fire, and his Holy One a flame, and it will burn and devour his thorns and briers in one day." Isaiah 10:12-17)

It would be easy to apply this passage to an historical event, but upon closer scrutiny of the text, we find evidence of something more. While in Isaiah's time Assyria was a present and terrible threat to Judah's security (II Kings 18:13), neither he nor any of the other historic kings of Assyria were dealt with in a single day, and certainly not by the "Holy One" of YHVH. This is certainly a Messianic prophecy, the details of which extend into the future. Doubtless the Assyrian king Sennacherib was a type of the coming man of sin of whom the prophecy was made.

The following chapter, Isaiah 11, is a continuation of the prophecy discussing the peace that will rule the Day of the Lord when YHVH's kingdom will be established upon the earth. This peace is the direct result of the Messiah's advent and His destruction of the Assyrian, a condition of prophecy spoken of by the Apostle Paul:

"Remarkably, Paul cites this Assyrian text from Isaiah when he describes the death of the Antichrist at the hands of the returning Messiah (II Thess. 2:8). It is difficult to resist the conclusion that Paul saw in the evil ASSYRIAN of Isaiah 10-11 the final antichristian tyrant. We have no difficulty in recognizing Paul's quotation of Isaiah 10:22, 23 in Romans 9:27, 28 — "the remnant will return" — as a prophecy of the future restoration of Israel. There is no good reason to overlook his quotation of the destruction of the ASSYRIAN as the destruction of the eschatological antichrist. The "114 — 228 connection" (Isa. 11:4; II Thess. 2:8) deserves careful examination. The secret of much good Bible study is discovering the links between the Old and New Testaments. Most mistakes occur when the connections are broken, especially when the Old Testament is neglected. Much of traditional Christian orthodoxy is based on a Greek philosophical reading of the New Testament severed from the Old" [3]

While the prophecy of the 10th chapter of Isaiah is compelling in itself, it is further bolstered in the oracle concerning Babylon beginning at 13:1. In language that clearly speaks of the last days, YHVH's army will be the ultimate fulfillment of which the Media Persian Empire was a type. While history affirms that the mighty city of Babylon did fall into their destructive hands, it was many years later that its ignoble state was attained not by war, but by the ravaging fingers of time and the desert sands of Mesopotamia. Babylon was moved some time later by the Greek general Seleucus I Nicator near the present day site of modern Bagdad, after which the original site slowly fell into disrepair and obscurity, eventually being swallowed up by the unrelenting Mesopotamian sands. A city is not just a bunch of buildings, but rather the people who dwell within its boundaries.

It should be noted that the Babylonians and their king will play a major role in the oppression of the nation of Israel in the last days in that when he is defeated and they are at peace, they will take up a taunt against him. This is the majority of the text of the 14th chapter. He is spoken of in terms that also fit the king of Assyria:

"How you are fallen from heaven, O Day Star, son of Dawn! How you are cut down to the ground, you who laid the nations low! You said in your heart, 'I will ascend to heaven; above the stars of God I will set my throne on high; I will sit on the mount of assembly in the far reaches of the north; I will ascend above the heights of the clouds; I will make myself like the Most High." (Isaiah 14:12-14)

Although used by a great many expositors as a proof text for the rise of Satan, the above passage is actually about the Beast who will meet his end at the Messiah's appearance. The king of Babylon and the king of Assyria are one and the same. This can be verified through at least five things.

First, the Babylonian king's relevance to the recovered nation of Israel is an issue that must be investigated. If the Assyrian king is the one who will cruelly subjugate Jacob almost to the point of complete annihilation, why then would they take up a taunt against Babylon's sovereign? Throughout their history, they have had many despotic foreign rulers that oppressed them and culled their numbers, but none that could meet the stature and intensity of the coming Beast. If there was ever an individual who merited such a verbal memorial, it would certainly be him.

Second, as the above text reveals, the Babylonian king will be a boastful man whose ambitions reach all the way to God's throne. This is clearly the one defining characteristic of the Antichrist:

"I considered the horns, and behold, there came up among them another horn, a little one, before which three of the first horns were plucked up by the roots. And behold, in this horn were eyes like the eyes of a man, and a mouth speaking great things." (Daniel 7:8)

"Let no one deceive you in any way. For that day will not come, unless the rebellion comes first, and the man of lawlessness is revealed, the son of destruction, who opposes and exalts himself against every so-called god or object of worship, so that he takes his seat in the temple of God, proclaiming himself to be God." (II Thessalonians 2:3, 4)

"And the beast was given a mouth uttering haughty and blasphemous words, and it was allowed to exercise authority for forty-two months. It opened its mouth to utter blasphemies against God, blaspheming his name and his dwelling, that is, those who dwell in heaven." (Revelation 12: 5, 6)

The Beast is a braggart. He will attain a certain and great amount of power (given to him by the Almighty One to his own hurt) and spend a fair amount of time proclaiming it in the ears of others. He wants to be God, overthrowing angelic powers (Daniel 8:9).

Third, his boast is that he will sit on the mount of the assembly, i.e. the mountain of Jebel al-Aqra. Among the Semitic people of Ugarit on the shore of the Mediterranean, there was the belief that the gods assembled on Mt. Zaphon, also known as the mountain of Baal. The passage here speaks of it being in the far reaches of the *north*. Zaphon is the word used indicating the mountain, but not necessarily the direction. Incidentally, Mt. Zaphon is just to the north of the city of Antioch, home of the Grecian kings of the Selucid dynasty.

Fourth, he is also a spiritual being. He is called the Day Star, son of Dawn. The appellation of Star is used in scripture of angelic beings (Judges 5:20, Job 38:7), and we know that the Beast too is an angelic being and will ascend out of the bottomless pit (Revelation 17:8). The spiritual being will possess the body and drive the will of a man to do many unspeakable things. He will overthrow the power and position of some other angels (Daniel 8:8, 9).

A brief word should be said here concerning this passage. It is very often used as a proof text for Satan's character and, taken out of its context, gives that appearance. The title *Day Star* (Hebrew, HEYLEL) is translated in some Bible versions as *Lucifer* which is a transliteration from the Latin Vulgate, and as a consequence became the assumed name of the adversary, Satan. Lucifer is not the name of the devil. This text is not about man's accuser, but about the *man of sin,* who is also possessed by an angelic being who is to come at the end of this age.

Lastly, the two kings are treated as one and the same:

"I will rise up against them," declares the LORD of hosts, "and will cut off from Babylon name and remnant, descendants and posterity," declares the LORD. "And I will make it a possession of the hedgehog, and pools of water, and I will sweep it with the broom of destruction," declares the LORD of hosts. The LORD of hosts has sworn: "As I have planned, so shall it be, and as I have purposed, so shall it stand, that I will break the Assyrian in my land, and on my mountains trample him underfoot; and his yoke shall depart from them, and his burden from their shoulder." (Isaiah 14:22-25)

The oracle given by Isaiah was on Babylon and its king, which finishes with their destruction in which YHVH declares that He will break the *Assyrian* in His land. The swift and seamless transition from Babylon to Assyria is certainly not due to a change in subject matter. There is no announcement of another oracle, just the concluding remarks of YHVH's plan. This raises the obvious question: Why would two separate nations be seen as one?

In ancient times people would group together according to ethnicity. This is to be expected, as each nation had their own language or regional dialect. Assyrians and Babylonians, though geographically near neighbors and shared the same pantheon of gods, as well as both Semitic in origin, had their own distinct territories. Their histories are replete with periods of domination and subjugation, conquering and being conquered. In modern times, however, maps and boundaries are mostly drawn up along political agendas. A given nation could be comprised of many diverse ethnic groups united under a single government. This is what I believe will be the situation at the end of this age. The nations of Assyria and Babylon bordered one another in ages past, but are now united under one political administration, the modern nation of Iraq which in modern times has changed governments several times.

Even though a politically based state may explain how the two leaders are seen as one, it is the Assyrian king who is mentioned the most in the Messianic prophecies. Ethnically, there is every possibility that he will be Assyrian, although virtually all of Assyrian descent are professed Christians. This fact alone may indicate that he could be an apostate Christian that has converted to Islam. Or he at least may come from its ancient capital, Nineveh, and there is some evidence of this from prophetic scripture.

The small book of Nahum is a prophecy on the seat of the Assyrian Empire. It tells of the greatness of YHVH and His judgment on the wicked city. In a somewhat cryptic passage it speaks of one who is to come from there:

"From you came one who plotted evil against the LORD, a worthless counselor. Thus says the LORD, "Though they are at full strength and many, they will be cut down and pass away. Though I have afflicted you, I will afflict you no more. And now I will break his yoke from off you and will burst your bonds apart." The LORD has given commandment about you: "No more shall your name be perpetuated; from the house of your gods I will cut off the carved image and the metal image. I will make your grave, for you are vile." (Nahum 1:11-14)

"Your shepherds are asleep, O king of Assyria; your nobles slumber. Your people are scattered on the mountains with none to gather them. There is no easing your hurt; your wound is grievous. All who hear the news about you clap their hands over you. For upon whom has not come your unceasing evil?" (Nahum 3:18,19)

Who is this king, this "worthless counselor"? The prophecy concerns the city of Nineveh, which historically reached its pinnacle of power and influence during the Neo Assyrian Empire. The prophecy could indicate Sargon I who plundered Israel, taking the nation into an ignominious exile, or perhaps later when Sennacherib came against Judah, but failed to take Jerusalem and conquer Hezekiah. However, the passage from the 3rd chapter seems to point to that coming time when the king of Assyria will fall on the mountains of Israel (Ezekiel 38:21).

The city of Nineveh still exists, though it has changed. The modern city of Mosul, Iraq, partially sits upon the ruins of the ancient metropolis with a population of two million inhabitants, and it is from this location that the Assyrian will most likely come. It is also the home of what remains of the dwindling Assyrian people.

The apocalyptic character of Ezekiel chapters 38 and 39 is well known among Bible scholars, both Jewish and Christian. An evil ruler by the name of Gog of Magog will muster together a coalition of nations and attack the nation of Israel. The identity of Gog and his land of Magog has been a debated topic in modern times. Is he an Oriental or perhaps Russian, Caucasian or Semitic? Is he the *man of sin,* or simply just another sinful man? Where is Magog? When will the time of his attack happen? All pertinent questions indeed!

For some years now the most commonly held belief, especially among evangelicals, is that Gog will be of possible Russian descent and that Magog is the land north of the Caucasus Mountains in what is currently southern Russia. In recent years, however, this has been proven false in light of historical and archaeological findings, and many diligent scholars are now coming to grips with it.

Through the cuneiform Royal Assyrian court records discovered in the last century, we find mention of a Lydian king referred to by the Greeks as Gyges who was also mentioned by Herodotus in his *Histories.* He is called in the Assyrian language Gugu Ludu, Gyges of Lydia. Hebrew, being also a Semitic language, would thus call him Gog of the land of Gog (Magog). He lived and had his influence about a hundred years before Ezekiel's time and was known for his building a military coalition of nations including Meshech, Tubal, and Beth-Togarmah ~ the very nations which the Beast will employ. Was he in fact the Gog of which Ezekiel prophesied?

Most likely it was him and the prophet was using him as a type of the coming man of sin, a pattern of a well-organized and efficient military strategist. While Gyges is now well dead and gone, he left us an example of one from the northernmost parts of the then known world of how nations can be united in a common goal, in this case the invasion of Israel in the last days. The coming Beast will be the Assyrian and the king of Babylon from the area of modern day Iraq. He will be a type of Gyges, Sennacherib, Antiochus Epiphanies, Hitler and other powerful men of old.

- The Beast is both a kingdom and a king.
- He will be possessed by a demonic spirit which will ascend out of the bottomless pit.

- He will appear as the Muslim Mahdi and the False Prophet as Issa (Jesus).
- He will be the king of both Assyria and Babylon.

THE THIRD TEMPLE

It is believed by many students of eschatology that there will be a third Temple constructed, as there is some evidence in both the Old and New Testaments that such a structure is forthcoming (Daniel 9:26,27; Matthew 24:15; Mark 13:14; 2 Thessalonians 2:4; Revelation 11:1). I, however, as of this writing am not 100 % certain that a Temple proper, i.e. a permanent edifice built of stone, is going to be built, but then again I could be wrong. My thinking on the matter follows two avenues.

First, while there is mention in the scriptures of a future Temple, it is scant in number; only five or six places, depending on one's interpretation. This lack of attention seems odd considering its importance to God's prophetic plan. Is this deficit of references significant? At this point in time, I honestly don't know, but this fact certainly raises my suspicions and curiosity enough to warrant further inquiry.

The language used is also revealing. Throughout the New Testament there are two Greek words used for the Temple. The first is HEIRON used of the structure itself. It includes all outwardly visible parts of the building as well as the surrounding courts. When Jesus was taken by Satan to the pinnacle of the Temple and tempted to test the Fathers willingness to protect His Anointed, this is the word used (Mark 4:5; Luke 4:9). HEIRON is always indicated for the laity accessible part of the Temple, not the restricted areas for the priests and purified workers.

The second word is NAOS and is used of the sanctified parts, the area that makes the Temple what it is: A Holy Place. In Acts 19:24, it is used when a silversmith named Demetrius stirred up the people of Ephesus against the Apostle Paul and the gentile converts who had come to the faith in that city. He made shrines (NAOS) for the goddess Artemis and the growth of the faith was cutting into his business. NAOS therefore designates the object or area of holiness. It is this word that is used in all the New Testament passages for the future Temple.

In the Hebrew, we find a similar distinction between the structure as a whole (HEYKAL, palace, building; and BEIT, house) and the sanctified area (KHODESH, holy (place)). The Holy Place is further divided between the Holy (KHODESH) and Most Holy (KHODESH KHODESH). The Hebrew doubles the word to express the superlative. In Daniel 9:26, speaking prophetically, it tells that the people of the prince (Antichrist) who is to come will destroy the city and the Holy (KHODESH) Place. It is further attested to in the Greek LXX by TO HAGION (the holy). Interestingly, Jesus referred to the Holy Place (TOPO HAGIO) in Matthew 24:15 rather than call it the Temple.

It is these two things, the lack of references and the words used that prompted me to entertain the idea that perhaps a *permanent* building for a Temple might not come about in these closing days of this age. How then could there be a Holy Place if there is no Temple? Or even better how could there be a Temple without a Holy Place? Actually there is a way to fulfill all the scriptural requirements concerning the Holy Place either with or without having to build a permanent structure.

The second Temple in the 1st century was a magnificent structure. Though it began as a modest building that was nowhere near as glorious as the first Temple built by Solomon (Haggai 2:3), it later (under the auspices of Herod the Great) was expanded and improved to become a massive edifice that was admired by all nations. This improvement stage took 46 years and became so associated with the Idumean king that it is in modern times often referred to as Herod's Temple.

Great as that structure was in its heyday, it was essentially, however, an empty shell. Missing from its Holy Places was the one thing that YHVH gave to His chosen people that was an integral part of the Law given by Him to Moses. That one thing that was so necessary to the ritual ceremonies of the Temple, was in fact the one thing it was based upon, the Tabernacle and its very heart, the Ark of the Covenant.

The Tabernacle (Hebrew MISHKAN, from the root meaning to sit or dwell) was used in the service of YHVH up till the time that Solomon built Him a permanent house (1 Kings 6:1), at which time it was brought up and placed under the carved wooden cherubim inside the Most Holy Place (1 Kings 8:4). The tent itself was consecrated to YHVH and nowhere in the scriptures is it said to be decommissioned. It is certain that they did not just throw it out in the trash heap. The whole of the sacrificial service was based upon the Mishkan because it is a shadow and type of the heavenly reality, therefore its importance could not be negated. So what would be done with a sacred relic that is still viable?

I see two possibilities. The tent could have been destroyed by fire in a Holy Place, much like the red heifer sacrifice (something of which the scriptures don't even hint), or it could be folded up and stored away, which to my way of thinking would be the logical thing to do. Because it is sanctified, it would not be kept just anywhere. It would of necessity have to be protected and separated from light, moisture, and movement.

The most logical place to store the Tabernacle that comes to my mind is within the Most Holy Place of the house of YHVH. The dimensions of the temple that Solomon erected are given in 1 Kings chapter 6. The Most Holy Place was a room 20 cubits square, in which the whole Tabernacle fully assembled would have been able to fit inside. We know from the scriptures that at the dedication of YHVH's House, that the staves of the Ark of the Covenant, the poles used by the priesthood to bear it about, protruded and were seen outside of the Most Holy Place (1 Kings 8:8). The staves which were never to be taken out of the Ark (Exodus 25:15) were able to fit inside the much smaller inner sanctum of the Tabernacle without any difficulty, so why the protrusion? Either they were replaced with longer ones at some time since the exodus of the children of Israel from Egypt (unlikely), or the Ark was placed further East toward the entrance of the Most Holy Place. What reason could we find for placing the Ark so close to the entrance? Did the builders of the Temple miscalculate the necessary space for it?

Obviously, the Temple builders knew what they were doing when they undertook such a grand task. The blueprint for the job came via God's Spirit to David the king, Solomon's father (1 Chronicles 28:11, 12). Upon initiation of the project Solomon enlisted the aid of Hiram, king of Tyre, who sent him a very skilled man, also named Hiram, who worked with the Israeli craftsmen in all areas of the work (2 Chronicles 2:12-14). Could not the storage of the Tent of Meeting in the back of the Most Holy Place force the placement of the Ark to be somewhat moved?

There are many mysteries in our world: Bigfoot, the Loch Ness monster, how the great pyramids were built, etc. But the greatest, I believe, is over the fate of the Mishkan and the Ark of the Covenant. The Ark is a wooden chest overlaid with gold that at one time contained the stone tablets of the Ten Commandments that Moses made and that YHVH wrote upon. It originally occupied the Most Holy Place in the Tabernacle that accompanied the children of Israel through their wilderness journey to the promised land of Canaan. It, along with the Tabernacle, was later placed in the first temple that Solomon erected in Jerusalem. Where they went from that point on, the scriptures leave a silent witness. They do, however, tell us of the sacking and destruction of Jerusalem and the Temple in 586 B.C.E. by the Babylonian king Nebuchadnezzar. It has been surmised by some that they were carried away to Babylon along with all the Temple treasures, but to that end there is no proof.

Besides the obvious assumption of Babylonian extraction, there are other claims made by men that the Ark of the Covenant exists today. Some believe that it resides in a small heavily guarded church in Axum, Ethiopia protected by an African branch of the Orthodox Church. There are certain adherents to a doctrine known as British Israelism that hold that the Ark is buried under an ancient coronation stone on a hill top in Ireland. Others still hold that the Ark was taken away to foreign lands such as South Africa, France, or even America.

Although the scriptural canon is silent in its regard, there is the apocryphal book of II Maccabees that states that Jeremiah the Prophet prior to the invasion of Jerusalem took the Ark, Mishkan, and the Tabernacle furniture from Solomon's Temple and proceeded to carry it toward Mt. Nebo, and in route he came upon a cave wherein he hid them (II Maccabees 2:4-8).

Beginning in 1947, fragments as well as whole ancient documents were found by Bedouins in the caves around an ancient Essene village, today known as Khirbet Qumran. They are known to the world as the Dead Sea Scrolls. These documents revealed many of the day by day rituals and regulations of the relatively unknown sect, as well as some prophetic writings found in the Hebrew canon. Among the artifacts retrieved were two copper scrolls found by a combined Dutch/Jordanian archeological expedition in 1952.

The copper scrolls measured approximately seven feet long and were in such fragile condition that they could not be unrolled for fear of damaging them. They remained in that state for a couple of years till Professor H. Wright Baker of the College of Technology at Manchester, England carefully split them in half with a small circular saw and gently flattened the halves, revealing the writing that was inversely punched into the sheets. What was revealed has baffled scholars for decades. It appears to be a treasure map of sorts, containing cryptic directions to large amounts of buried gold, silver, and gems. The language is a straight forward form of Hebrew similar to Mishnaic writings with an orthography that, according to more than one expert, *appears* to date from the mid-to-late first century C.E.

In 1648, Danish Rabbi Naphtali Ben Elchanan wrote a kabalistic book entitled *Emek Ha Melek* (valley of the king) which mirrored the account of II Maccabees, but also told of the recording of the deed on a copper sheet (which was not discovered until 1952!). Among the treasures said to be hidden was the Ark of the Covenant as well as the Mishkan and its furniture. How did he know of such a thing unless it was by special revelation, or (most probably) it was related to him through oral tradition? At any rate, the coincidence is uncanny as well as eye-opening.

The copper scrolls while being legible were, however, unintelligible. That is until a retired fireman from Apache, Oklahoma named Jim Barfield used his award winning investigative powers to decipher its hidden references. After petitioning the Almighty One for wisdom and insight, he discovered within a few short minutes the truth of the scrolls: The directions are based on geographical and manmade structures excavated at the Essene community. I have communicated with Jim on several occasions and am convinced that he has in fact solved the greatest mystery in the history of the world. At the time of this writing, his group, the Copper Scroll Project, has successfully performed ground penetrating radar tests showing the presence of large amounts of non-ferrous metals at the sites in question. I firmly believe that the Mishkan and its furnishings will be excavated and revealed to the world in and around the ruins of Khirbet Qumran soon, perhaps as early as the year 2016.

So what, one may ask, will the discovery of the Ark of the Covenant have to do with the price of eggs in China? How does it affect the salvation of those who are seeking after God? In a direct sense, it doesn't. At the risk of sounding sacrilegious, the Ark is physically nothing more than a gold covered box with no intrinsic power of its own. The writer of the book of Hebrews tells us that the Tabernacle and all its appurtenances are a type and shadow of the spiritual reality:

"Now the point in what we are saying is this: we have such a high priest, one who is seated at the right hand of the throne of the Majesty in heaven, a minister in the holy places, in the true tent that the Lord set up, not man. For every high priest is appointed to offer gifts and sacrifices; thus it is necessary for this priest also to have something to offer. Now if he were on earth, he would not be a priest at all, since there are priests who offer gifts according to the law. They serve a copy and shadow of the heavenly things. For when Moses was about to erect the tent, he was instructed by God, saying, "See that you make everything according to the pattern that was shown you on the mountain." (Hebrews 8:1-5).

They are a physical picture and representation of a greater and efficacious spiritual reality. Am I saying that anyone can approach and handle it without any danger or harm? Absolutely not! Its existence at the end of this age is not without purpose or plan. The Ark is the physical repository for the tablets that Moses hewed out of stone and YHVH wrote on supernaturally. It represents YHVH's throne and righteousness which is in heaven and should be feared and respected. What then is its significance in the coming days?

Israel, like any other society, is a divided one upon certain socio-political values; not all Israelites are Torah practicing Jews. This is reflected in their oft changing parliamentarian form of government. While there is a clear ultraconservative element among the people, it's in the minority. Most Jewish citizens of Israel appear to be less than gung-ho in expanding the territory to the extent of its former Davidic kingdom glory. Finding the Miskan and Ark would surely throw a monkey wrench into the works and accelerate the desire of the ultra-conservative Jews to rebuild the Temple. This in itself presents a major problem.

It is reckoned by most scholars that the site of the Al Aqsa mosque on the Haram esh Sherif sits, at least in part, upon the location of the former Temples of Solomon and Herod. This area, known as the Temple Mount, although being in the Jewish controlled city of Jerusalem, is not controlled by the state of Israel, but by the Islamic Jordanian organization called the Waqf. The discovery and recovery of the "heart of the Law" will most probably bring about a period of intense bloodshed as the Muslims consider it a threat to Islam's third most holy site.

This, I believe, can possibly be averted by building the Temple on its proper historical location approximately 700 feet to the south of the present retaining wall on property already owned by Jews in the Jewish quarter of the old city. This discovery was made by the late Earnest L. Martin in the 1990's and presented in his book *The Temples that Jerusalem Forgot*. Martin was a brilliant historian who once oversaw a large archeological excavation in the old city.

Regardless of whether they build on the Haram esh Sharif or south of it, the result will probably be the same: War. The recovery of the Mishkan bears witness to Israel's claim that the land is their heritage given by God, and the Islamic extremists of the surrounding nations will have none of it. This therefore will be a prophetic fulfillment, as the land is spoken of as having been brought back from the sword (Ezekiel 38:8).

A major result of recovering the Ark of the Covenant is that the whole world to a certain degree will be affected. Jerusalem, and especially the Temple site, is highly esteemed by Christians, Muslims and Jews the world over, and there are extremists among them all who would limit access to the others. Any move made by the Jews to erect a Temple regardless of its location will have repercussions the world over.

Prophetically speaking, I am now of the opinion that the discovery will spark a conflict that will allow the nation of

Israel to utilize the Ark for their protection. What else would cause the many surrounding Islamic nations to sue for peace? The scriptures speak of the man of sin confirming a covenant only to possibly break it at a later date:

"And after the sixty-two weeks, an anointed one shall be cut off and shall have nothing. And the people of the prince who is to come shall destroy the city and the sanctuary. Its end shall come with a flood, and to the end there shall be war. Desolations are decreed. And he shall make a strong covenant with many for one week, and for half of the week he shall put an end to sacrifice and offering. And on the wing of abominations shall come one who makes desolate, until the decreed end is poured out on the desolator." (Daniel 9:26, 27)

This covenant, which will be for a period of seven years, will see the abolition of the sacrificial system in the Temple at its mid-point. It is commonly held among Biblical scholars that the prince will uphold a covenant of peace with Israel for this time frame, but that is not entirely clear. Does he strengthen this agreement with the Israeli's, or is the agreement between him and the other (the *many* v. 27) Islamic nations? The Hebrew in the above passage does not directly state or imply that the abolishing of the Temple oblation by the prince is a violation of the agreement. At any rate the scriptures seem to indicate that Israel will be at peace and safely dwelling in the land.

Fear of the God of Israel, or perhaps, more correctly, a superstitious fear of the Ark (a common misconception is that the Ark will bring victory to *anyone that it proceeds in battle*) may possibly have a psychological effect on the Arab peoples of the Levant. This may come about by a seeming miraculous defeat of their armies when engaging

Israel. It may also be that Israel will become complacent believing that the Ark will protect them. This has happened before in their history.

During the days of Samuel the Prophet, the children of Israel went to war with their perennial enemies, the Philistines. At their first skirmish, Israel received heavy losses of about 4,000 men (1 Samuel 4:2). Dejected and upset at their initial defeat, they regrouped and, without consulting their God, they presumptuously went and got the Ark and brought it into the camp. The next battle was a disaster; 30,000 Israeli men died and the Ark which the Elders of Israel thought would save them from their enemies was captured and brought back to Philistine territory (1 Samuel 4:10-11). Their primary mistake wasn't just a tactical error in the field, but was in failing to consult the Lord. Because as a people they were allowing the idolatrous worship of false gods, He was angry at them and withdrew His support. Only after they repented and put away their idols were they capable of garnering a victory in war (1 Samuel 7:1-4). I am of the opinion that a similar thing could happen again for the offspring of Jacob at the last days of this age.

The scriptures are clear that the Lord will use the "Assyrian" (Isaiah 10:5) to punish His wayward children, and for them the result will be disastrous. It will be the time known as "Jacob's trouble" (Jeremiah 30:7) and is the Great Tribulation. The land will be plundered and a third of the population will be left, many to be taken away and sold as slaves as the rest are killed (Zechariah 13:8). This will give occasion for the Assyrian ruler to desecrate the Most Holy Place and possibly use the Ark as his throne.

"Let no one deceive you in any way. For that day will not come, unless the rebellion comes first, and the man of lawlessness is revealed, the son of destruction, who opposes and exalts himself against every so-called god or object of worship, so that he takes his seat in the temple of God, proclaiming himself to be God." (2 Thessalonians 2:3, 4)

CHAPTER FOURTEEN: A LOOK TO THE END

The 14th chapter is a breaking point of sorts for the book. Heretofore, the action *appears* to be building toward a climax, although in actuality it was reached at the beginning of the 8th chapter (opening of the seventh seal) and again at the end of the 11th chapter (sounding of the seventh trumpet). Now what we see is the 144,000 Israelites from chapter 7, only this time *after* the Tribulation from which they were sealed. After which, we also see the proclamations of three angels and two separate but related harvests. These all share the same timeframe, near the end of the Great Tribulation.

As I previously stated in this book, the Revelation is composed of many short, rapid scenes that contribute to a difficult interpretation. The seeming morass of minor characters and actions all contribute, in one way or another, to the overall theme that the Almighty will triumph in the end while making the journey there a problematic one. This literary minefield can effectively and easily be traversed by observing this one little but simple rule: In almost every instance where the writer uses the terms *then I saw, after this I looked*, or one of its variants, the scene almost always changes altogether, often starting at the beginning of the books timeframe, 3 ½ years, the beginning of the Great Tribulation. Hence, we find at the opening of this chapter a completely different subject matter from the previous 13th chapter, a look at the Beast and his False Prophet. Had we assumed that the book was in a chronological order, we would once again be faced with an interpretive conundrum. The last plagues of the bowls of wrath are yet to be poured out on the Beast and his followers, yet the Lamb and His followers are seen upon the earth, on Mount Zion, in obvious triumph. By the use of this small rule, we can make light appear amidst the darkness of the blatantly cryptic subject matter.

These Israelites are symbolically representative of all the saved who went through the Great Tribulation. Thus, they are able to sing a new song -one of victory through redemption- before the four living creatures and the Elders. This is a song that all the redeemed of all ages can share in. We can be certain of this because the scriptures tell us that none can learn it but those who will be redeemed from the earth (14:3) and from among mankind (14:4). In other words, all who have walked the earth, which are God's elect that will take part in the first resurrection (20:6).

These redeemed followers are seen on Mt. Zion along with the Lamb. For those that take a literal and linear approach to the book, they are met with a chronological challenge of Biblical proportions; Jesus Christ, the conquering king, doesn't show up with the army of God until the 19th chapter. Are we to suppose that He is going to cool His heels at Jerusalem till the last series of plagues is poured out upon the Beast and then begin to take action with the sword? Clearly, in order to make sense, one must take a proleptic stance which destroys the literal interpretation of the passage. The import at this point of the book is that those who will place their trust in the Anointed

One of God will find rest and triumph over the evil of this world.

The next section of subplots concerns three angels with three distinct messages. This of course is perfectly in keeping with the Almighty's *modus operandi* as His spirit's primary work is that of couriers; they shuttle information to His children and others (Hebrews 1:14).

"And I saw another angel fly in the midst of heaven, having the everlasting gospel to preach unto them that dwell on the earth, and to every nation, and kindred, and tongue, and people, Saying with a loud voice, Fear God, and give glory to him; for the hour of his judgment is come: and worship him that made heaven, and earth, and the sea, and the fountains of waters." (Revelation 14:6, 7)

The first angel mentioned is a herald to every nation on earth of God's impending judgment. The language is such that this should be taken literally. An actual angel will be speaking in the hearing of all mankind, which indicates to us that this is to take place at the *end* of the Great Tribulation. In this age, God deals with mankind through mundane means and common methods. It may be that He sends a cataclysmic storm as a judgment on certain people, but it has always appeared as a natural force, never as a supernatural occurrence. But on this occasion, there will be an angel addressing the world, something unheard of. In the past, they have spoken to individuals as well as groups of people. Something upon hearing others could possibly doubt, but when all the inhabitants of earth experience it there will be none to question the Almighty's existence or interest in mankind.

Another proof that this falls at the tail end of the 3 ½ years of plagues is seen in the name of the judgment itself, the *hour* of judgment. This is no blanket statement or generalized prophecy; it is a specific time ordained by the Father. So many things will happen in that short span of time that I dubbed it *high noon* in my studies: Showdown time like in the old western movies, God's family of the righteous resurrected saints led by Jesus against the rest of mankind deceived and mobilized by Satan and the false messiah, the Muslim Madhi. These two groups will clash in an epic battle like no Hollywood movie could ever portray. It literally will be a blood bath that will reach to the horse's bridles (14:20).

In my lifetime, I've encountered many errors that well minded but often mislead people cling to in lieu of sound doctrine. These errors are usually glaring misconceptions based upon relatively unimportant details that are misinterpreted or simply glossed over. All that said, people are going to accept and believe only in what they are willing to invest their faith. One such doctrine among evangelicals is that of the rapture of the church. It is based upon an ambiguous and weak doctrine concerning the true hope of all believers, the resurrection of the dead.

When asked, all of those who adhere to the rapture doctrine can't give you a clear definition concerning the raising of the dead. How many resurrections are there? And if more than one, when do they occur? And even more importantly, what scriptural proof is there in which to base said doctrine? My observation is that although the doctrine is part and parcel of the resurrection, its emphasis, especially by dispensational evangelicals, is on escape from this world. Its timing is coincided with a "secret" return of Jesus in the air only, something at which the scriptures never even hint of. A key verse in the Revelation that many teachers use as support for it is Revelation 3:10:

> "Because you have kept my word about patient endurance, I will keep you from the hour of trial that is coming on the whole world, to try those who dwell on the earth."

Here, we have what seems to be a promise of escape for Christ's faithful servants, and indeed it is. That this is a promise there is no doubt, but what exactly are we looking at? I see two issues that must be addressed in order to glean any truth from this passage. First, the preposition used concerning the hour of trial is, in my opinion, poorly represented by our English word *from*. The Greek preposition EK found in the original text is a word that carries the idea of that which comes *out of the midst*. This actually gives the meaning that He will take the faithful believer *out of the midst* of the trial, something in which the person must first be found. This alone precludes any possibility of a pre-Tribulation escape.

Secondly, and still more important to this discussion, is the exact definition of the trial. It is assumed by many, if not practically all dispensational evangelicals, that this is a reference to the Great Tribulation which I assert that it is not. What it is referencing is a specific hour, a short increment of time at the end of the Tribulation, during which God, represented by His agent in this world, Jesus the Christ, will, after having gathered representatives of all the nations together, confront mankind in an epic showdown. The Old Testament prophets time and again spoke of this coming event with amazing clarity and consistency, but it wasn't until John penned the revealing truth in the book of Revelation that it was collated and became available for us to see in detail.

"Remember, then, what you received and heard. Keep it, and repent. If you will not wake up, I will come like a thief, and you will not know at what *hour* I will come against you:" (Revelation 3:3)

"So the four angels, who had been prepared for the *hour*, the day, the month, and the year, were released to kill a third of mankind." (Revelation 9:15)

"And at that *hour* there was a great earthquake, and a tenth of the city fell. Seven thousand people were killed in the earthquake, and the rest were terrified and gave glory to the God of heaven." (Revelation 11:13)

"And he said with a loud voice, "Fear God and give him glory, because the *hour* of his judgment has come, and worship him who made heaven and earth, the sea and the springs of water." (Revelation 14:7)

"And another angel came out of the temple, calling with a loud voice to him who sat on the cloud, "Put in your sickle, and reap, for the *hour* to reap has come, for the harvest of the earth is fully ripe." (Revelation 14:15)

"And the ten horns that you saw are ten kings who have not yet received royal power, but they are to receive authority as kings for one *hour*, together with the beast." (Revelation 17:12)

"They will stand far off, in fear of her torment, and say, "Alas! Alas! You great city, you mighty city, Babylon! For in a single *hour* your judgment has come." (Revelation 18:10)

"For in a single *hour* all this wealth has been laid waste." And all shipmasters and seafaring men, sailors and all whose trade is on the sea, stood far off and cried out as they saw the smoke of her burning, "What city was like the great city?" And they threw dust on their heads as they wept and mourned, crying out, "Alas, alas, for the great city where all who had ships at sea grew rich by her wealth! For in a single *hour* she has been laid waste." (Revelation 18:17-19)

It will be seen that the hour mentioned is more than just a figure of speech meant to represent a general time of judgment. It is a specific increment of time where all of God's plan comes together harmoniously in order to usher in His Kingdom on earth. During that hour, many things will happen, some very bad, but ultimately the lasting good of His plan will triumph. There are a few major events that will take place during the hour, the order of which is a matter for speculation.

Earthquakes are a common feature in many areas of the world; due to geological features, some localities experience them on an almost regular basis. There are, however, historically speaking, places that rarely, if ever, have them. That is, until recent years. Due to several variables (some of which are perhaps even manmade), the world has recently witnessed an increase of quakes in areas not known for them, and people are experiencing them for the first time in their lives. Jesus foretold of this phenomenon. In what is known by Bible scholars as the Mount Olive discourse, He predicted that "nation will rise against nation, and kingdom against kingdom, and there will be famines and *earthquakes* in various places" (Matthew 24:7, see also Mark 13:8 and Luke 21:11). These He added, were, however, just the beginning of the "birth pains," a figure of speech that is used in the scriptures to denote the Great Tribulation, the time leading up to the birth of God's Kingdom on earth (Jeremiah 6:24, 13:21, 30:6,7; Micah 4:9).

The scriptures also speak of another quake far stronger and more destructive than any that has ever happened on earth:

"And there were voices, and thunders, and lightnings; and there was a great earthquake, such as was not since men were upon the earth, so mighty an earthquake, *and* so great. And the great city was divided into three parts, and the cities of the nations fell: and great Babylon came in remembrance before God, to give unto her the cup of the wine of the fierceness of his wrath. And every island fled away, and the mountains were not found." (Revelation 16:18-20)

"And the same hour was there a great earthquake, and the tenth part of the city fell, and in the earthquake were slain of men seven thousand: and the remnant were affrighted, and gave glory to the God of heaven." (Revelation 11:13)

"And I beheld when he had opened the sixth seal, and, lo, there was a great earthquake; and the sun became black as sackcloth of hair, and the moon became as blood; And the stars of heaven fell unto the earth, even as a fig tree casteth her untimely figs, when she is shaken of a mighty wind. And the heaven departed as a scroll when it is rolled together; and every mountain and island were moved out of their places." (Revelation 6:12-14)

"Therefore I will make the heavens tremble, and the earth will be shaken out of its place, at the wrath of the LORD of hosts in the day of his fierce anger." (Isaiah 13:13)

"The earth quakes before them; the heavens tremble. The sun and the moon are darkened, and the stars withdraw their shining." (Joel 2:10)

"For thus says the LORD of hosts: Yet once more, in a little while, I will shake the heavens and the earth and the sea and the dry land." (Haggai 2:6 see also Hebrews 12:26)

This coming earthquake will be like no other, even moving every island and mountain out of their places. No small feat! Such a quake will so disrupt daily life that it will be practically impossible for mankind to recover their civilized infrastructure for many years; the digging out alone may last weeks, if not months. The human race will be decimated. Communications will all but cease, and the need to find food and clean water will come first. Isaiah foretold that men would become more scarce than fine gold, as rare as the gold of Ophir (Isaiah 13:12).

If we are to correctly read the Old Testament prophets, this quaking is to be coincident with the approach of God's army. The prophet Joel, speaking of the Day of the Lord, tells of how His army will approach the land to annihilate the northern enemy and bring deliverance to His people. The power and devastation that they will yield will cause the land before them to appear as the Garden of Eden in contrast:

"Blow a trumpet in Zion; sound an alarm on my holy mountain! Let all the inhabitants of the land tremble, for the day of the LORD is coming; it is near, a day of darkness and gloom, a day of clouds and thick darkness! Like blackness there is spread upon the mountains a great and powerful people; their like has never been before, nor will be again after them through the years of all generations. Fire devours before them, and behind them a flame burns. The land is like the Garden of Eden before them, but behind them a desolate wilderness, and nothing escapes them. Their appearance is like the appearance of horses, and like war horses they run. As with the rumbling of chariots, they leap on the tops of the mountains, like the crackling of a flame of fire devouring the stubble, like a powerful army drawn up for battle. Before them peoples are in anguish; all faces grow pale. Like warriors they charge; like soldiers they scale the wall. They march each on his way; they do not swerve from their paths. They do not jostle one another; each marches in his path; they burst through the weapons and are not halted. They leap upon the city, they run upon the walls, they climb up into the houses, they enter through the windows like a thief. The earth quakes before them; the heavens tremble. The sun and the moon are darkened, and the stars withdraw their shining. The LORD utters his voice before his army, for his camp is exceedingly great; he who executes his word is powerful. For the day of the LORD is great and very awesome; who can endure it?" (Joel 2:1-11)

There can be no doubt that Revelation 6:12-17 is a mirror image of this passage of scripture:

"When he opened the sixth seal, I looked, and behold, there was a great earthquake, and the sun became black as sackcloth, the full moon became like blood, and the stars of the sky fell to the earth as the fig tree sheds its winter fruit when shaken by a gale. The sky vanished like a scroll that is being rolled up, and every mountain and island was removed from its place. Then the kings of the earth and the great ones and the generals and the rich and the powerful, and everyone, slave and free, hid themselves in the caves and among the rocks of the mountains, calling to the mountains and rocks, "Fall on us and hide us from the face of him who is seated on the throne, and from the wrath of the Lamb, for the great day of their wrath has come, and who can stand?"

What we are looking at is clearly the climax of the age. The nations have been gathered together, there is a massive earthquake, and the Almighty within the personage of the Anointed One, Jesus, leading His army will make His appearance upon the earth as men observe in horror the outpouring of His wrath. The passages both end in the same rhetorical exclamation: Who can endure/stand it?

This brings us to the battle itself, universally called the battle of Armageddon, a misnomer as there is no pitched battle in that precise location. What the scriptures tell us is that the leaders of the nations will be gathered there. The armies of the nations, primarily Islamic ones, will literally fill the land of Israel. The nations will be gathered together in the land primarily as the result of lies told by Satan, the Beast, and the False Prophet (Revelation 16:13, 14), although it is the Lord who has predetermined to bring them all together (Zephaniah 3:8, Zechariah 12:3). What transpires after that is a slaughter of immense proportions. John wrote that the blood from God's winepress will reach unto a horse's bridle (14:20) to a distance of 1600 stadia or roughly 180 miles. This will happen outside the city of Jerusalem. Some critics could very well point out the impossibility of such a scenario, but a closer look at the conditions on that day will shed some further light.

The Levant has a diverse topography. It varies from plain to mountain quickly in a short distance; it is very hilly. In his prophecy, Zechariah mentions that on the Day of the Lord the city of Jerusalem will be elevated above the surrounding land, which due to the great quake will be flattened as a plain:

"The whole land shall be turned into a plain from Geba to Rimmon south of Jerusalem. But Jerusalem shall remain aloft on its site from the Gate of Benjamin to the place of the former gate, to the Corner Gate, and from the Tower of Hananel to the king's winepresses." (Zechariah 14:10)

This leveling of the land will doubtless have some irregularities, i.e. low spots, which can conceivably be filled with the blood of slain men to a depth equivalent to a horse's bridle. Jerusalem itself will be a very tall mountain. In fact, it will be chief among all mountains:

"It shall come to pass in the latter days that the mountain of the house of the LORD shall be established as the highest of the mountains, and shall be lifted up above the hills; and all the nations shall flow to it," (Isaiah 2:2, Micah 4:1)

Jerusalem will become the capitol of the world, so that all nations will come and worship God and His Anointed. Elevated above everyone and everything the shekinah, God's presence in the form of a great shining light, will be a beacon to all men. It is conceivable that everyone on that side of the globe will be able to see its light in the night sky.

The Army of God who will bring about this great slaughter is seen in the 19th chapter of Revelation:

"Then I saw heaven opened, and behold, a white horse! The one sitting on it is called Faithful and True, and in righteousness he judges and makes war. His eyes are like a flame of fire, and on his head are many diadems, and he has a name written that no one knows but himself. He is clothed in a robe dipped in blood, and the name by which he is called is The Word of God. And the armies of heaven, arrayed in fine linen, white and pure, were following him on white horses. From his mouth comes a sharp sword with which to strike down the nations, and he will rule them with a rod of iron. He will tread the winepress of the fury of the wrath of God the Almighty." (Revelation 19:11-15)

The armies of God are His newly resurrected people, the Bride of Christ. This is seen by their attire: Fine linen, white and pure which is the righteous deeds of the saints (Revelation 19:7, 8). We who are God's people *are* the troops spoken of in Joel. The 149th Psalm is a very revealing passage as to the saint's role in the coming battle:

"For the LORD takes pleasure in his people; he adorns the humble with salvation. Let the godly exult in glory; let them sing for joy on their beds. Let the high praises of God be in their throats and **two-edged swords in their hands, to execute vengeance on the nations and punishments on the peoples, to bind their kings with chains and their nobles with fetters of iron, to execute on them the judgment written!** This is honor for all his godly ones. Praise the LORD!" (Psalm 149:4-9) (Emphasis mine)

As His soldiers, we who are the resurrected children of faith will literally take the sword and annihilate the millions of people who stand to oppose the Lord of the whole earth.

The second angel (14:8) proclaims a coincident event: The fall of the "Mystery" Babylon. This fall is not that of a rebuilt ancient metropolis as many have surmised. It is tempting to identify this Babylon with the Beast's kingdom which will be comprised of the old dominions of Assyria and Babylon, but I am reticent to accept such identification. This subject will be dealt with in chapters 17-18.

The third angel (14:9) sums up the judgment of God by declaring the end result of His punishment: Torment in the fire and brimstone of the lake of fire (14:10). This is to be meted out upon those who have actively thrown in their lot with the Beast. In verse 11, many proponents of a spiritual hell will find support for their belief due to an unfortunate and erroneous reading. The first part describes the finality of the sinner: Smoke and ash which will not be quenched, but allowed to burn out on its own (Mk 9:48; Is. 66:24; Mal. 4:3). The last half describes the current situation of those who accept the Beast. They are suffering the plagues of the seals, trumpets, and bowls both day and night, with no respite or rest.

At this point in the chapter, John interjects, over the angelic pronouncement, the necessity of perseverance in righteousness by the believer as also mentioned in conjunction with the Beast in 13:10. The salvation of man requires faith on the part of the recipient and not merely a onetime pronouncement of their belief or the submission to a ritual such as baptism, and those caught in the Tribulation of those days will have their faith tried even unto death.

In the 13th verse there is a curious statement concerning the death of all the elect from that point onward:

"And I heard a voice from heaven saying, "Write this: Blessed are the dead who die in the Lord from now on." "Blessed indeed," says the Spirit, "that they may rest from their labors, for their deeds follow them!"

The meaning of this passage will make perfect sense to the reader once they factor in the preceding verses. John has just revealed the culmination of YHVH's plan: The resurrection of the righteous dead and the mustering of them in the final battle of this age. From that point onward, into the next thousand years, those elect who will transpire will immediately be transformed and clothed with that incorruptible body (1 Corinthians 15:53, 54; ll Co. 5:1, 2; Romans 8:23) which the elect of this current age will have already received.

From this, the scene once again changes with the words "after this I looked," and we see an illustration of the Messiah (one like a son of man, with a golden crown on his head) sitting on a cloud who dutifully reaps the earth at the command of God's messenger from out of the Temple because the *hour has come*. It should be clear from the previous content of the chapter that the object of this reaping will be the righteous saints who will be taken out of the world just before the hour of temptation.

Coincident to this is seen another harvest, wherein a heavenly messenger gathers grapes, which represent YHVH's wrath, and casts them onto the earth, which is YHVH's great winepress. Both of these happen at the same time. As the Lord explodes in righteous indignation at the disobedient inhabitants of the earth, He simultaneously protects His beloved children from harm. Isaiah foresaw this very thing:

"Your dead shall live; their bodies shall rise. You who dwell in the dust, awake and sing for joy! For your dew is a dew of light, and the earth will give birth to the dead. Come, my people, enter your chambers, and shut your doors behind you; hide yourselves for a little while until the fury has passed by. For behold, the LORD is coming out from his place to punish the inhabitants of the earth for their iniquity, and the earth will disclose the blood shed on it, and will no more cover its slain." (Isaiah 26:19-21)

CHAPTER 15: SECOND OVERTURE

In the last chapter, there was mention of an interpretive rule concerning scene changes. Nowhere more necessary and significant is the use of the rule than in the 15th chapter, for its simple employment clarifies much and facilitates the learning process greatly. Chapters 4 and 5 were an overture that introduces the reader to a major purpose of the book: Declaring the fitfulness of the Messiah as YHVH's only agent to bring upon the earth the Great Tribulation, represented as the scroll sealed with seven seals.

In this chapter is announced (v. 1) the enactment of the *last* seven plagues, in which the THUMOS (intense wrath) of YHVH finds its completion. Here again, I must caution the reader to consider the cryptic style in which the letter was composed; they are the last plagues for those following the form and not the content of the book. In light of this, we should recognize that we are essentially back at the start of the action because the seals, trumpets, and bowls happen concurrently, thus making it a second overture.

After the brief introduction, the scene rapidly changes from the start of the action to the finish with the words "and I saw," where we see those resurrected saints who persevered and overcame the Beast and his trials, the image and the mark, against their faith (vs. 2-4). These conquerors are witnessed singing praises and the song of triumph ascribed to both Moses and the Messiah. Due to the rapid change of scenarios, it is easily seen how the reader could get confused.

The allegorical language aside, we can be certain that the saints represented are not merely seen as disembodied spirits in the heavenly realm. Whatever the meaning of the various elements, there is absolutely no scriptural evidence that people exist in the spiritual world, much less carry musical instruments in their hands. This passage is obviously allegorical and should not be taken literally.

Again in the 5th verse we apply the rule, and the action shifts back to the beginning and we see the Holy Place (NAOS) in heaven opened and messengers of the Lord bearing the seven judgments, leaving the sanctuary to deliver their awful contents. The Holy Place is then filled with smoke from YHVH's glory, so that no one will be able to enter to either offer incense or prayer. This obstruction is due to man sinning away his day of grace. Once the judgment of the Lord begins, there is no stopping it until His anger relents. The whole of chapter 16 is the continuation of this passage.

THE TALE OF TWO WOMEN

In the 12th chapter we were introduced to a group of people identified as the children of a Woman seen in heaven. They are the true believers, i.e. the elect, both those who will escape persecution from the Antichrist in the Levant and those unfortunate ones who will suffer and pass through the fiery trial of the Great Tribulation. She is seen as a righteous lady who gives birth to a king who is to "rule the nations with an iron rod" (no doubt a reference to Jesus Christ). She in fact is the personification of the future city New Jerusalem.

In contrast, chapter 17 introduces us to another but different woman: A vile licentious Harlot who has spawned others like unto herself, the infamous Whore of Babylon, who also corresponds to a city. What or who is she and who are her children, and what city does she represent?

It is my conviction that the book of Revelation, along with its obvious subject of the coming Day of the Lord, has an underlying opposite but just as obvious theme: That there are evil systems at work in the world that are destined to be destroyed on that day. We have already seen a political one throughout mankind's history represented by the seven headed Beast; the Whore is a religious one which rides on top of it.

She is introduced to the reader as sitting upon many waters which the text reveals to be peoples, multitudes, nations, and languages (17:15), which highlights her universal influence. She is definitely a multinational coalition of peoples. In the mid-nineteenth century, a Presbyterian minister named Alexander Hislop published a tome long respected by Protestants entitled *The Two Babylons*. In it, he identified the Roman Catholic Church as the Whore, citing archeological and historical evidence that it was the ancient worship of Baal handed down through the ages, and although some of the proof he presented has been negated through modern archaeological findings, he was never the less *partially* correct. The Roman church has in its organization pagan religious doctrines that originated with ancient Babylon, and upon simple casual observation it can easily be seen that it fits the description.

However, while I agree he was right to point the finger at the church of Rome, he didn't go far enough in separating the pagan influences from the truth. To understand this we must ponder the origin of the mystery. The woman bears upon her forehead the name Mystery Babylon (17:5). This is a point of contention among expositors. Should it be rendered Mystery Babylon or mystery, Babylon? Is it a part of the title or just a descriptive introduction? I think that it should be understood as a descriptive part of her title. She is being introduced as a secret form of government, one hidden in plain sight of all. Government is simply the control of people. Organized religion is also a form of people control. The two systems, while different, accomplish much of the same goal.

It is a common mistake of Bible scholars to confuse this Babylon with the modern Babylonian kingdom of the Mahdi. Many have thought to make the Babylon of the 17th chapter a literal treatise on the demise of the ancient but revived city on the Euphrates. There is, to my mind, little doubt that some of the Old Testament prophecies concerning the city should be taken literally. They were in fact talking about the fall of an actual empire and city, the seat of the coming Assyrian.

The modern archaeological consensus is that Mesopotamian culture began around the fourth millenium B.C. in the land of Sumer and ascribes to it the invention of writing, as well as the origin of the Semitic pantheon which governed the faith of the Babylonians and Assyrians. It is currently held that the southern city states of Sumer predated that of those Semitic peoples located north between the rivers who are often described as marauding, uneducated vandals that absorbed their higher societal culture. This is patently false.

The secular bias of the academics that were largely responsible for the excavations and publishing of the kingdoms of "the cradle of civilization" saw the Sumerians, Assyrians, and Akkadians as distinct primitive peoples who migrated from other parts and settled in the fertile plain watered by the Tigress and Euphrates rivers. They were partially correct. The descendants of Noah did in fact migrate from the region of Ararat (Gen. 11:1, 2), but as *one people* united by a single language. Their distinctions lie in the fact that were divided, both linguistically and physically, by a singular experience that changed the way men perceived one another's speech, the confusing of man's speech at the tower of Babel (confusion) in the city of Babylon (gate of God [Akkadian]).

But the Babylon spoken of here is also figurative. Hence the name, Mystery Babylon. She is being revealed to the reader as something that was heretofore hidden. The city was an actual site on the plain of Shinar (Sumer) where the rapidly growing population of the post-flood society emigrated:

"Now the whole earth had one language and the same words. And as people migrated from the east, they found a plain in the land of Shinar and settled there. And they said to one another, "Come, let us make bricks, and burn them thoroughly." And they had brick for stone, and bitumen for mortar. Then they said, "Come, let us build ourselves a city and a tower with its top in the heavens, and let us make a name for ourselves, lest we be dispersed over the face of the whole earth." (Genesis 11:1-4)

This story is well known to even the youngest Sunday school student. The people who descended from Noah wanted to stay together, so they began erecting a tower and city whose top would reach into the heavens. The Lord however finds fault with the plans of mankind and takes action to scatter them in spite of their attempt at unification:

"And the LORD came down to see the city and the tower, which the children of man had built. And the LORD said, "Behold, they are one people, and they have all one language, and this is only the beginning of what they will do. And nothing that they propose to do will now be impossible for them. Come, let us go down and there confuse their language, so that they may not understand one another's speech." So the LORD dispersed them from there over the face of all the earth, and they left off building the city. Therefore its name was called Babel, because there the LORD confused the language of all the earth. And from there the LORD dispersed them over the face of all the earth." (Genesis 11:5-9)

Was it that God didn't want men to build towers? Obviously that in itself is no sin. What actually transpired was much more insidious than mere masonry work. The text reveals that the Lord was concerned with their unification above all things. As they begin to do such things as one people, then nothing could be held from them. They intended to build a tower to make a "name" for themselves.

From the scriptures we see that from ancient times a title or name carried authority. Just as today to speak or act in the name of someone or something is to do it with power; the person acting becomes the agent of the other. In this case, they sought to create their own authority - essentially their own god – and begin their own unified government.

This was nothing less than a rejection of the progenitor of the human race. Figuratively speaking, men have been building towers and rejecting the one true God ever since.

The key to this passage was that they were attempting to do it universally, as one people and organization. Because they were dispersed and their plan thwarted, Satan, the one that moved them to do it, later moved to "go in the back door" by creating a shadow government: Religion. This "universal" or "Catholic" organization is built upon three tenets: 1) The concept of multiple gods, 2) the belief in an afterlife or immortality of man's soul/spirit, and 3) the teaching of an eternal punishment to keep the ignorant and unenlightened masses in order. A cursory study of the major faiths of this world will reveal these three principles are truly universal (at least in part, if not completely). Islam and Judaism with their staunch monotheism are the lone exceptions.

The Mystery Babylon has been alive and well throughout history, albeit hindered by God's scattering of mankind back at the tower. This is why I reject the idea that the "man of sin" will head up a one world government. YHVH didn't allow it back in the early days after the flood, and He won't allow it at the end of this age. This attempt at control of the masses has ridden on the backs of human governments since those days, just as the Harlot rides on the seven headed Beast.

So what exactly is the Whore? It is a pagan religion that permeates societies the world over and was present during the reigns of the seven kingdoms represented by the Beast's seven heads. It exists today reincarnated as Catholic (universal) Christianity of which the Roman Catholic Church, a universal church that seeks to make all its adherents part and parcel of its reach and control, is its best example. Unfortunately, in the eyes of the world, the

Vatican represents Christianity. It is clearly not Christian in its teachings, doctrines, and actions as can be seen throughout the so called "church" history.

She is described as being clothed with purple and scarlet and adorned with gold, jewels and pearls (17:4), which bespeaks of great wealth. It would be naive to think that organized "Christian" churches are not run on money. The annual budgets of a great many individual congregations run in the millions of dollars, even more so an institute such as the Roman church with over a millennium of prospering at the expense of the poor, so that even a blind man can see that the church at Rome is extremely wealthy. A passing look into its holdings reveals a disturbing amount of riches which translates into power and authority.

The Harlot is pictured holding in her hand a gold cup filled with abominations and immorality, and she commits fornication with the kings of the earth (17:2). Although the universal church has had its periods when it could not prosper in the face of certain human governments (the French Revolution with its humanism easily comes to mind), it has always survived and thrived growing even larger and more influential. Fornication is the compromising of the integrity of the flesh; the Apostle Paul said that it is a sin against one's own self (1 Corinthians 6:18). The fornication that it carries out with the kings of the earth is the compromising of principles and morality, which it does whenever it serves its purpose. The modern world's history is permeated with the intrigue of the Roman church. It has used its influence to shape the political landscape in multiple societies.

It is the mother of harlots in that it, through its missionary endeavors, has gone about to make disciples of like faith and order. Even the wayward Protestant churches (her children), though attempting to distance themselves from its hierarchy, have carried with them the universal false doctrines. Many of the mainline Protestant churches that once taught that salvation is by God's grace through faith have abandoned that teaching as well. All these are in error of the truth: That there is but one God, the Father, that man is a physical being and not an immortal soul. The concept that there is but one church and that all Christians, regardless of their denominational leanings, are a part of it is just false. True believers have never been a part of the Roman church, the Whore of Babylon. This is nowhere more evident than in its persecution of the righteous saints.

She is intoxicated with the blood of the saints, the witnesses of the Savior (17:6). To deny Rome's role in the persecution of the saints is equivalent to denying that the Jewish holocaust of World War II ever happened. The atrocities that many of the Popes sanctioned against believers are well documented, and it has been estimated by several Protestant sources that as many as 50 million souls perished during the Dark Ages. While I personally believe that that number of deaths is grossly overestimated, the fact remains that it is responsible for the deaths, both directly and indirectly, of countless men, women and children. History tells of torture by fire, water and dismemberment, the stake, pike and auto-da-fé, the Roman Inquisition, the Spanish Inquisition and the Crusades. In no way are these actions those of the Bride of Christ whose white raiment represent the righteousness of the saints (19:8). Christians are to be known by their love (1 John 3:18).

At this point, it should be obvious that the great city that the Whore personifies is Rome. It has, because of the false church within it, ruled over many kings of the earth, and it was the great city of the empire in John's day; the whole of 18th chapter deals with its demise. The ten horns are ten

Islamic nations aligned with the Mahdi (17:12, 13). They, being devout monotheists, hate the Whore, whom it is presumed is the representative of Christianity to the world, and will attack and burn Rome (17:16, 17) because they consider Christians to be heretics.

In summary, I must point out that the Roman Catholic Church (universal) never was "the church" that was started by our Lord on the shores of the Sea of Galilee. The true church is a local, visible congregation made up of two or more people who profess a belief in God and accept Him through His Son, Jesus Christ, and have followed up their faith by submitting to the ritual of baptism. They exist scattered among the various denominations and in their spiritual actions are answerable only to the head of their local bodies: Christ. The true church is not found in a hierarchy, as this was explicitly forbidden by its founder (Matthew 20:25-28).

THE FALL OF BABYLON

"After this I saw another angel coming down from heaven, having great authority, and the earth was made bright with his glory. And he called out with a mighty voice, "Fallen, fallen is Babylon the great! She has become a dwelling place for demons, a haunt for every unclean spirit, a haunt for every unclean bird, a haunt for every unclean and detestable beast." (Revelation 18:1, 2)

In the previous chapter, I identified the Roman Catholic Church as the best candidate to represent the Whore of Babylon. I hold that it is not only the organization per se that is evil, but the universal doctrines that it purveys as also found in the majority of "Christian" faiths. These doctrines were absorbed from Greek philosophy starting around the second century A.D. But behind the Greek philosophy is a mythology with an historic path leading through Canaanite and Phoenician cultural ties with the ancient Semitic peoples of Mesopotamia. The world is a much smaller place, culturally speaking, than what we may suppose. The major religious tenets held universally had their origin in the early centuries after the flood in the plain between the two rivers.

The Whore, being both a city and a belief system, finds its incarnation in the Roman church, which the nations of the world quite mistakenly equate with the organization that Christ began during His ministry. Hated by Islam, along with Judaism, it will become the recipient of anger by their messiah the Mahdi, who with a coalition of ten nations *will burn her with fire* (Rev. 17:16). What will transpire on that day is the end result of an all-out religious war, a jihad; a resurgence of hostilities like that which took place in medieval times, the Crusades.

Actually the jihad against Christians and Jews has been ongoing ever since the rise of Islam. The Assyrian and Nestorian Churches, whose influence historically reached as far as Japan, has been all but destroyed from Muslim persecution rangeing from mild economic pressure to intense military eradication. The demise of millions of Christians throughout Asia and Africa was directly due to its fervent missionary zeal which continues even unto today. This persecution is ongoing largely due to the newfound wealth and influence (which translates into power) of several Arab nations generated from crude oil production.

Also in this day, there seems to be a myriad of radical Islamic groups of varying degrees that all share the same basic ideology: Hatred of Israel and the Christian West. These mostly Arab groups have historically warred with one another. During the Crusades, some Muslim kings actually allied with their Christian enemies in order to topple their rivals. These states of constant warfare have always been due to greed and ambition among the rulers and lack of focus of the people. What will bring them all together in the soon coming days is the rise of the Mahdi with his wonder producing False Prophet, Issa.

The Prophet Daniel foresaw much in regards to the Mahdi and his role during the last 3 ½ years of this age. In the visions that YHVH granted him, the coming man of sin was seen as a horn of diminutive size (Daniel 7:8), leaving us with little doubt that he is to be a minor character that will ascend rapidly to the acme of power. This was also true of Adolf Hitler who was known to be a laggard that only made the rank of a corporal in the army before his skills in oration catapulted him into Germany's seat of power. Likewise, the Mahdi will be identified by his great boasting rhetoric (II Thessalonians 2:4; Revelation 13:5).

Daniel revealed the Mahdi in the type of Antiochus Epiphanies (Daniel 11:31-36), who swept through the land of Israel and desecrated the Temple in Jerusalem by offering swine's flesh on its altar to the god Jupiter. In his day, he was opposed by ships of the emerging Western power of Rome, causing him to vent his anger out on the Jewish people and their covenant with YHVH. In the 11th chapter of the book of Daniel beginning at verse 40, we can see a change in the vision:

At the time of the end, the king of the south shall attack him, but the king of the north shall rush upon him like a whirlwind, with chariots and horsemen, and with many ships. And he shall come into countries and shall overflow and pass through. He shall come into the glorious land. And tens of thousands shall fall, but these shall be delivered out of his hand: Edom and Moab and the main part of the Ammonites. He shall stretch out his hand against the countries, and the land of Egypt shall not escape. He shall become ruler of the treasures of gold and of silver, and all the precious things of Egypt, and the Libyans and the Cushites shall follow in his train. But news from the east and the north shall alarm him, and he shall go out with great fury to destroy and devote many to destruction. And he shall pitch his palatial tents between the sea and the glorious holy mountain. Yet he shall come to his end, with none to help him. (Daniel 11:40-45)

As can be seen above, the time is set as that of the end. The king of the south (most probably Egypt) will attack the king of the north. Why? What circumstance or reason could bring about such an action? Daniel revealed that at the rise of the little horn, three of the ten horns belonging to the fourth beast would be ripped up by the roots (Daniel 7:8). The horns all represent kings, but who are they, and what is the significance, if any, of the three?

I believe that the three horns are modern day equivalents to the three empires which preceded the fourth beast/empire that Daniel wrote about in chapter 7. They are portrayed as a loin, bear, and leopard and coincide with Babylon, Media–Persia, and Greece. These three would be the modern day nations of Iraq, Iran, and Syria. Babylon would be Iraq, Persia is Iran, and Syria, which was once the western-most dominion of the Grecian empire. This also matches the description of the Beast in Revelation 13:2. Remember, the Beast is *both* a kingdom and a king. The ten would then represent ten Islamic nations that will receive authority along with the Beast in the final hour of this age (Revelation 17:12, 13).

There are any number of reasons why a nation such as Egypt would provoke another Islamic one into an armed conflict. It could be over boundaries, resources, ideologies, or, as I think in this case, a combination. Islam, like so many others, is a divided faith. The two divergent branches, Sunni and Shite, have a long and troublesome history of hostilities spanning back to the 7th century. In the years after the death of Mohammed, two factions sprang up: The majority favoring a leadership by the Caliphates under the succession of Abu Bakr (Sunni), his father-in-law, the other those in the line of Ali, his son-in-law and the third Caliph (Shiite). The animosity and rivalry of these two sects is extremely bloody.

At the time of this writing, it would appear that the Shiites which are the majority in the nation of Iran, are making in-roads into Iraq and the Palestinian people through terrorist organizations such as Hezbollah bent on destroying both the Sunni's and Israel. It is a known fact that Iran is responsible for state sponsored terrorism. I believe that it is entirely possible at this time, and in the coming days, that the Beast may well ascend to power in the present nation of Iraq, being aided by Shiites from Iran and others to become a coalition which will invade the south into Egypt. There are some indications in the scriptures that point to such a scenario. Of course, the king of the south may attack the Beast in retaliation for his overthrow of the three kings.

When the Beast (of whom Gog is a type) invades the lands of the Levant, the modern day nations of Iran, Ethiopia, Libya, and Turkey will support and take part in the attack (Ezekiel 38:5, 6; Daniel 11:43). This leaves us with the current nations of Syria, Lebanon, and Iraq, which are currently involved in civil conflicts, unaccounted for. Egypt will fall, but the Saudi's, Yemenites, and Jordanians will not be overtaken (Ezekiel 38:13; Daniel 11:41). If Saudi Arabia falls to this force, the scriptures don't reveal it. Along with Sheba (Yeman) and Dedan (Saudi Arabia), Tarshish, who many assert to be a Western nation such as the U.S., will enquire as to their intentions: "Have you come to seize spoil?" This doesn't sound like a defeated country. It also doesn't point to a one world government which the majority of Bible scholars believe that the Beast will head.

Once he is ensconced in Israel he will enact his own version of sharia law and his troubles will soon begin. The plagues that the Two Witnesses bring upon both the whole world and, specifically, his kingdom will begin to wear down him and his people, while simultaneously hardening their hearts, just as the ten plagues did to Egypt in the time of the exodus. As these plagues begin to soften up his forces and the other nations of the world become angry with him, he will hear and be alarmed at news from the north and east, quite possibly Russia, India, and China. As Antiochus did in the past, so he will do, seeking to annihilate all the elect and stamp out the infidel Christian and Jewish influence in his dominion. As the forces from the north and east begin to close in on him, he and his ten nations will attack the (supposed) heart of Christianity: Rome, home of the Roman Catholic Church.

At no time am I declaring that the Mahdi will be accepted at first by all Muslims. The fact that the Saudi's and Yemenites appear to be opposed to and untouched by his military advances may indicate that his influence is not initially universal. It could also be that they will opt not to challenge him and remain neutral. At any rate, they aren't taking an active role in his campaign. The heart of Islam is its holy site in Mecca which is controlled by the house of Saud and is under the auspices of Wahhabism, so it doesn't seem likely that they would remain indifferent to his advances. If the man of sin is in fact seen by the Muslims as the Mahdi, then it would stand to reason that the Saudis will embrace him and also proclaim, "Who is like the beast, and who can fight against it?"

It would be prudent in this regard to consider the motives of the ten horns. Why would they, being political entities, hate a religious one with such ferocity? Does it not seem likely that they will be Muslims and that they hate the power and universal influence that the Roman Catholic Church wields over the nations of the world? Christianity is still the largest faith upon the face of the earth and, try as hard as many do, you simply can't separate religion from government. This is why I believe they will incinerate Rome. They will be thinking they are eradicating a false and apostate faith and its influence in world affairs.

They will burn her with fire. Considering the meteorological circumstances at the end of the Great Tribulation period and the logistical requirements to field an army or armies into a theater, it makes perfect sense that the mode of destruction will be nuclear. This would account for the response of them standing far off for her torment (Revelation 18:10). In the final hour of this age, mankind will unleash the fury of their anger upon one another, so that upon the dawning of the Day of the Lord, man will be as scarce as the gold of Ophir (Isaiah 13:12).

CHAPTER 19: THE SEVENTH STEP

It is in the 19th chapter that the content and form, the literal and figurative, come together. The whole purpose and intention of the letter written to the churches of Asia Minor finds its fulfillment here. Not only is it the culmination of the letter, but also the message of the Bible overall.

In this chapter, there are three things that will happen as the Day of the Lord begins to dawn. The first is the celebration of the Whore's demise – the death of false religion and the universal lie. The effect of her influence is the keeping of humanity in spiritual darkness that will cease on that day.

"Behold, is it not from the LORD of hosts that peoples labor merely for fire, and nations weary themselves for nothing? For the earth will be filled with the knowledge of the glory of the LORD as the waters cover the sea." (Habakkuk 2:13, 14)

In that coming age, the knowledge of the one and only true God will not be an issue to debate, but all will know that He exists and is the rewarder of them who seek after Him (Hebrews 11:6). Such a great and noble truth has been hidden in plain sight since mankind's fall in the Garden of Eden. As the Apostle Paul said, "If our gospel is veiled, it is veiled only to those who are perishing. In their case, the god of this world has blinded the minds of the unbelievers, to keep them from seeing the light of the gospel of the glory of Christ, who is the image of God" (II Corinthians 4:3, 4).

The Harlot's influence, not only from her death inducing lies, but also the actual blood spilling of the righteous, will once and for all be nullified. Her presence will be no more. She will no longer persecute the saints for following their God and Father. This is of course a continuation and the logical and obvious result of the destruction of that evil system seen in the previous chapter.

The second event will happen just mere moments before the great destruction. His Bride, all the saved throughout history, will be called out of this world through the power of His resurrection. All together we shall meet with Him in the air (1 Thessalonians 4:13-17; Revelation 3:10, 11:12, 18:4) and ever be with Him. This is the marriage of the Lamb. Marriage is the physical union of a man and woman, and in the resurrection all the saved of all ages will be united in their flesh as one people with YHVH's anointed, Jesus, as the proxy groom of the Almighty One.

There are several different views espoused by scholars as to who the Bride is composed of at that day. Some hold that she will be the church, others are more specific maintaining that she will be a particular group of "Christians," and still others (like myself) that it will be made up of the saved of all ages. I hold this view due to my belief that God sees all men in black and white terms: Either you are a spiritual Jew or you aren't.

"For no one is a Jew who is merely one outwardly, nor is circumcision outward and physical. But a Jew is one inwardly, and circumcision is a matter of the heart, by the Spirit, not by the letter. His praise is not from man but from God." (Romans 2:28, 29)

What the Lord wants from men is repentance and faith toward Him. He does not want us to perish in our sins, but that everyone comes to Him (II Peter 3:9).

This group is extremely blessed. Having received the white robes of righteousness, they will be invited to join in the great feast of the Lamb that will take place at the mount of God, Jerusalem:

"On this mountain the LORD of hosts will make for all peoples a feast of rich food, a feast of well-aged wine, of rich food full of marrow, of aged wine well refined. And he will swallow up on this mountain the covering that is cast over all peoples, the veil that is spread over all nations." (Isaiah 25:6, 7)

"Then I looked, and behold, on Mount Zion stood the Lamb, and with him 144,000 who had his name and his Father's name written on their foreheads. And I heard a voice from heaven like the roar of many waters and like the sound of loud thunder. The voice I heard was like the sound of harpists playing on their harps, and they were singing a new song before the throne and before the four living creatures and before the elders. No one could learn that song except the 144,000 who had been redeemed from the earth. It is these who have not defiled themselves with women, for they are virgins. It is these who follow the Lamb wherever he goes. These have been redeemed from mankind as firstfruits for God and the Lamb, and in their mouth no lie was found, for they are blameless." (Revelation 14:1-5)

The third thing that the passage covers is built upon the resurrection of the righteous dead, a necessary event to the first two. The Lord Himself will lead His army, whose ranks are filled by the newly animated, each arrayed in bright white linen. This army will originate in the sky above the earth, and every one shall see Him and His hosts in their glory as they descend to the earth to accomplish the slaughter of kings and servants alike.

The Lord shall be arrayed in a robe dipped in blood sitting upon a white horse, the symbol of a victor and His name says it all: The Word of God. The picture presented is that of the very God Himself, YHVH, in the form of the Anointed. Just as the Father did by speaking the world into existence in creation, so will Jesus accomplish by the words which proceed from His mouth in destroying the hordes that have assembled against Him. He shall rule the nations of the earth with absolute authority, a rod of iron.

At His advent, the Beast and those nations under his influence will foolishly gather and prepare themselves to do battle. This exercise in stupidity will have but one result: The destruction of their armies and the capture and execution of their leaders, the Beast and the False Prophet, and after their wholesale butchering, their remains will be consumed by the birds of the earth (19:17). This is exactly what Ezekiel prophesied of concerning Gog of Magog in Ezekiel 39:17-20:

"As for you, son of man, thus says the Lord GOD: Speak to the birds of every sort and to all beasts of the field, 'Assemble and come, gather from all around to the sacrificial feast that I am preparing for you, a great sacrificial feast on the mountains of Israel, and you shall eat flesh and drink blood. You shall eat the flesh of the mighty, and drink the blood of the princes of the earth--of rams, of lambs, and of he-goats, of bulls, all of them fat beasts of Bashan. And you shall eat fat till you are filled, and drink blood till you are drunk, at the sacrificial feast that I am preparing for you. And you shall be filled at my table with horses and charioteers, with mighty men and all kinds of warriors,' declares the Lord GOD."

THE DAY OF THE LORD

All the action of the book finds its end in the 20th chapter. While it is not the completion of YHVH's plan, it is the last of the time ages. The thousand year age marked by a continuous day is the final ticking away of measured duration, as afterward it shall always be day. There will no longer be night or the need of heavenly bodies to set times and seasons (21:23-25; 22:5).

In the singular and glorious light of that day, Satan, who had been cast down from heaven, will be bound and cast into the bottomless pit from whence the Beast came (11:7, 20:1). The nations freed of his treacherous deceptions will exchange their weapons for farm implements and peace will reign from the King in Jerusalem (Isaiah 2:4; Micah 4:3).

This is the *last* day, the day that Jesus spoke about sandwiched between the two resurrections. It is during this period that the saints who have been reanimated will live and reign with their eternal king. Their occupation is to judge (1 Corinthians 6:2, 3) the aberrant angelic hosts and guide the nations (Isaiah 30:19-21), as they will be priests of God. Peace will reign and even nature will obey as the "wolf shall dwell with the lamb" (Isaiah 11:6).

The idyllic existence of that day, however, will not be perfect. Man, though isolated from his historic adversary, will still be born as a sinner and will have need of salvation. The salvation of that time will essentially be no different than it has been in the past ages: Willingness to accept the one true, invisible God, whose sole representative and ultimate agent is Jesus. Nevertheless, death will still come, and those sinners who die at our modern day advanced age of 100 years will be considered accursed (Isaiah 65:20). There will still be disputes among men, albeit under the watchful eye of the "Ruler with the iron rod" and His priestly servants (Isaiah 2:4).

After a thousand years, this structured and tightly controlled world order will come to an end, as Satan will be loosed from his prison for a short period in order to tempt and incite the nations of the earth to rebel against the Lord in Jerusalem (20:7), which will result in their annihilation. It is curious to note that even under that vigilant policing the majority of men will, when given the opportunity, amass as one people and take up arms in rebellion. Truly, the way is broad that leads to destruction and many shall follow that path (Matthew 7:13). This is part and parcel of YHVH's masterplan; He knows all His sheep and allows time and circumstances in order to bring them in from the wilderness to His sheepfold. Those who find their lot among those who will be destroyed will do so due to their own obduracy.

The mention of Gog and Magog (20:8) has caused confusion for some expositors. Some suppose this to be the same Ruler and people found in Ezekiel's prophecy (Ezekiel 38-39), of which it clearly cannot be. The quashing of that rebellion will result in a seven year period where the land's inhabitants will burn the weapons of war for fuel (Ezekiel 39:9, 10). This group will be destroyed by fire from heaven and go immediately to the White Throne judgment. Its reference here is due to its becoming a type of mankind's ultimate rebellion against God: Both king and people united as one.

Types play a huge role in God's word, often reinforcing truths in subtle yet profound ways. The whole of the Day of the Lord is a type and dress rehearsal of sorts as to what He plans to ultimately accomplish. The peace and harmony of that day, though forced, is a foretaste of the eternal bliss under which all of YHVH's children will come to live. Some of the similarities between that day and the ageless day that follows include never ending light, a river of life, and trees for healing.

Although the book of Revelation is the summation of YHVH's plan, the Day of the Lord and coming to earth of His eternal Kingdom, little is said about the day to day goings on of that time. This is actually covered more by the Prophets who wrote during the days before the Messiah's appearance. Isaiah saw many details that help us to understand.

Ezekiel's visions are also very precise. Chapters 40-48 are a record of that day with detailed measurements of the temple which the Messiah will build and directions for worship within it. Also included are directions as to how to divide the land among the tribes of Israel, and it is here that many will disagree with my controversial teaching.

Jesus, our blessed savior, was a man. He did not "come" to earth from a heavenly eternal existence, but was indeed 100% man, born of a woman and had a beginning similar to all others. True, His father was God, the Father, and through His all-powerful Spirit was begotten, but He was not spiritual, but biological, flesh and blood. He was one of us. He lived and taught and served God and His fellow man, but, more importantly, He died, something which God does not do. His resurrection was not of His own power, but of God who raised Him up:

Yet it was the will of the LORD to crush him; he has put him to grief; when his soul makes an offering for guilt, he shall see his offspring; he shall prolong his days; the will of the LORD shall prosper in his hand. (Isaiah 53:10)

By the so-called laws of nature, He should no longer exist or have a place among the living, yet He lives! Being resurrected and, I believe, as in Jesus' situation, deified doesn't make Him any less human but enhances his nature making it new and improved. Through His sacrifice which God accepted, He received a name and position far above all others and is worthy of our worship. Yet, He is still human, having the same endued psychological characteristics. He is, in fact, the perfect example of what all mankind could be if we only subjugate and suppress our sinful nature.

Underscoring His complete humanity, the Bible gives us a glimpse of how truly normal He is.

Isaiah, speaking of His appearance and ministry, used several titles to describe Him in Isaiah 9:6:

For to us a child is born, to us a son is given; and the government shall be upon his shoulder, and his name shall be called Wonderful Counselor, Mighty God, Everlasting Father, Prince of Peace.

These all have been debated and discussed from many different perspectives. The one that I want to briefly discuss is the title Everlasting Father. Among Biblical Unitarians, those that believe in the singular nature of God, the majority consensus is that it refers to Jesus' role of begetting spiritual children, i.e. being a spiritual leader much as a father would be to his children. While I concede that such an interpretation is certainly possible, it hinges upon the notion that the language used is meant to be taken figuratively. Of this, I'm not so sure. As I have stated before in this work, I am of the opinion that the scriptures often use both literal and figurative language at the same time in the same places. Direct your attention to the above passage from Isaiah chapter 53, where it says that He, referring to the Messiah, will see His offspring. There is no mandate from scripture that a man cannot marry and have children and fulfill his service to YHVH. Even the Apostle Paul who encouraged celibacy for service in the kingdom of God saw no sin in the institution but revered it (I Corinthians 7:6-8), as did the writer of the book of Hebrews (possibly Paul) (Hebrews 13:4). The modern day novel the *Da Vinci Code* that Jesus did father children but kept it secret, is unmitigated and unsubstantiated nonsense. Notwithstanding, there is in my thinking Biblical proof that He may indeed do so in the coming age.

The language of Ezekiel chapters 40-48 is quite literal and direct. In them, he describes the orientation of the coming temple, its services, and the distribution of the land to the children of Israel. Also found there is this eye-opening passage concerning the Prince of the land:

"Thus says the Lord GOD: If the prince makes a gift to any of his sons as his inheritance, it shall belong to his sons. It is their property by inheritance. But if he makes a gift out of his inheritance to one of his servants, it shall be his to the year of liberty. Then it shall revert to the prince; surely it is his inheritance--it shall belong to his sons. The prince shall not take any of the inheritance of the people, thrusting them out of their property. He shall give his sons their inheritance out of his own property, so that none of my people shall be scattered from his property." (Ezekiel 46:16-18)

The Prince may have sons! These are to be distinguished from His servants, who, if given a gift of the land, may keep it only until the year of Jubilee. There can be no doubt that these are living beings, flesh and blood people, for why would a resurrected person have need of a section of land? Also, it is clearly seen from the above verses that the Prince Himself is subject to the law of YHVH, which is exactly the position that the Messiah will also take (I Corinthians 15:27, 28).

It can definitely be ascertained that the Prince spoken of above is in fact the Messiah. In Ezekiel 37:21-25, there is ample confirmation of this truth:

"then say to them, thus says the Lord GOD: Behold, I will take the people of Israel from the nations among which they have gone, and will gather them from all around, and bring them to their own land. And I will make them one nation in the land, on the mountains of Israel. And one king shall be king over them all, and they shall be no longer two nations, and no longer divided into two kingdoms. They shall not defile themselves anymore with their idols and their detestable things, or with any of their transgressions. But I will save them from all the backslidings in which they have sinned, and will cleanse them; and they shall be my people, and I will be their God. My servant David shall be king over them, and they shall all have one shepherd. They shall walk in my rules and be careful to obey my statutes. They shall dwell in the land that I gave to my servant Jacob, where your fathers lived. They and their children and their children's children shall dwell there forever, and David my servant shall be their prince forever."

David here is portrayed as a type of the coming king Jesus. He is said to be king over them and that they will have but one shepherd, which is exactly what Jesus taught His disciples (John 10:16). In that coming time, David will not be raised up and placed on the throne of Israel, relegating Jesus to a role of second fiddle. David will take his place in the kingdom as all others will under the auspices and leadership of YHVH's Anointed One. To quell any possible argument to this interpretation, note that the titles of king and prince are used interchangeably.

This seemingly strange doctrine may appear to fly in the face of Jesus' teaching that those found worthy of that resurrection will not marry, but be as the angels of heaven (Matthew 22:30; Mark 12:25; Luke 20:34-36). It surely appears so, but rank has its privileges, and Jesus, though being a man, has earned the distinct advantage over all others. He told His disciples that He was going to lay down His life that He may take it up again (John 10:17, 18). Is not the life more than breath and blood? What about all the hopes and desires that one can naturally have? In the revealing light of the above passages, is not the simplistic humanity of Jesus brightly highlighted?

The Day of the Lord ends with the judgment of the unrepentant also called the White Throne Judgment. All those who ever existed and refused the Creator will be judged by His words (John 12:48; Romans 2:16) contained in the books that comprise scripture, the Bible. The memory of these souls will be erased as if they never existed (blotted out), as they are totally annihilated, body and soul, in the lake of fire (spoken of by the Lord as GEHENNA, Mt. 18:9; Mk. 9:43; Lk.12:5). Death's cold hand, both physical and figurative will also cease to be, leaving only vibrant life for all creation.

ALL THINGS NEW

After all these things have been fulfilled, the time of the world's reformation, which was foretold by the prophets of old, will come about. All of physical creation will be changed and made new; this is the revealed content of the 21st and 22nd chapters. As I discussed in the last chapter, the Day of the Lord is a type and dress rehearsal of this coming period, as they share some common elements.

The first is the light which the Lord will provide. Isaiah spoke of the light as a glory above Mt. Zion which will in that day be elevated above all other mountains (Isaiah 2:2, 4:5). Atop the mount will be the Temple, so the light will act as a beacon to the peoples of the world (Isaiah 60:1-3) to come to the house of the Lord.

In that coming ageless day, John foresees the New Jerusalem descending from heaven as a "bride adorned for her husband." Within it will be no Temple, as YHVH and His Anointed One shall dwell among mankind and themselves provide the light that otherwise would come from the sun and moon (21:22, 23). In that truly golden age, that pure light will be constant for the entire world, whereas previously it was over just the beloved land.

In typical Hebraic poetic fashion, the introduction of the Bride, the New Jerusalem, is seen twice (21:2, 10). The city is more than a structure or collection of buildings; it is also the people who make their homes there. The Bride is therefore both the city and the elect of God who have a dwelling within. This is also seen as the Woman observed in the 12th chapter.

The second element shared between the ages is the river of water of life that flows from the temple. In the former age, it will proceed from the threshold of the temple, while in the later age it flows from the throne of God and the Lamb. This water which is pure as crystal will bring life (Ezekiel 47:9) to all creatures that swim within it and will be available to all who are thirsty and who desire to drink, free of charge.

The final element they have in common are the trees that grow along the water's edge. In Ezekiel 47:12, the prophet noted that they were different varieties which drew their efficacy from the living water. They will bear their fruit monthly throughout the years, and their purpose there will be for the healing of people as it will also be in the final age, but with one difference: The tree of life with its twelve kinds of fruit will be the tree growing along that life giving stream (22:2).

"He who has an ear, let him hear what the Spirit says to the churches. To the one who conquers I will grant to eat of the tree of life, which is in the paradise of God." (Revelation 2:7)

CONCLUSION

The book of Revelation is quite simple to dissect and digest using the approach found in this book. While I have seen some other interpretations that are similar in scope, I have witnessed none that could tie all its particulars together with such clarity and purpose. The goal of the letter written to the seven churches is the Day of the Lord, His Parousia, or the advent of His kingdom on earth. These are little else than three different labels for the same event and its fulfillment is YHVH"s plan for man.

The beauty of His plan is seen in its exceptional simplicity: Seek out those people whom He foreknows shall willingly accept Him (read save) throughout the time ages with the intention of reanimating (resurrecting) and gathering them together under one Leader, chosen from among His fellow men (Jesus the Christ). This plan begins an age that lasts a thousand years, after which all who have rejected His offer of life and have died will also be resurrected and judged (White Throne judgment), then again remanded to death's domain in the lake of fire. Finally, death and the state of non-being (hell) will be abolished, and all those people and things will eventually be forgotten.

All these things He does for our sakes:

"Thus says the LORD: "As the new wine is found in the cluster, and they say, 'Do not destroy it, for there is a blessing in it,' so I will do for my servants' sake, and not destroy them all. I will bring forth offspring from Jacob, and from Judah possessors of my mountains; my chosen shall possess it, and my servants shall dwell there. Sharon shall become a pasture for flocks, and the Valley of Achor a place for herds to lie down, for my people who have sought me. But you who forsake the LORD, who forget my holy mountain, who set a table for Fortune and fill cups of mixed wine for Destiny, I will destine you to the sword, and all of you shall bow down to the slaughter, because, when I called, you did not answer; when I spoke, you did not listen, but you did what was evil in my eyes and chose what I did not delight in." (Isaiah 65:8-12)

As He revealed through Isaiah there are still some individuals left to redeem, *a blessing in the cluster*, and those willing of mankind still have time to attain that everlasting possession, but the time is drawing to a close. Examine your heart and motives and embrace the one true God.

ברוך יהוה

Blessed be the Name

CONCERNING DEATH

Concerning the matter of religion, the concept of an afterlife is truly universal. The majority of faiths, and every major one at that, all hold to the belief that man in some form survives death to continue his existence. As sacrilegious as it sounds, let us ask the question: Is there an afterlife?

Having a background in the Missionary Baptist Church, I was taught that man had one of two destinations: Heaven or hell. I blindly accepted this as if it was written in stone, but around the age of forty-five through a series of events, I began in earnest to look at the doctrine for the first time. Over a period of a couple of years, my thinking gradually yet radically changed. I slowly became convinced through the scriptures that the teaching of a spiritual existence apart from the body just doesn't happen. My journey began by defining exactly what we are as human beings.

If you were to take up the tools of a carpenter in order to build a house to live in, you would soon discover the importance of beginning with a level and square foundation. If the base is not true and equal in its dimensions, the walls and everything else up to the roof will not be either. All my life I've heard the terms body, soul, and spirit but had no concrete understanding as to their meaning, and that was unfortunate, because they are foundational to the proper understanding of true doctrine. Body is easy enough to figure out, but what is the difference between the soul and spirit? That they are two distinct things can be ascertained from how the scriptures use them. Over the course of my studies, I've asked minister friends their beliefs and opinions as to the difference and have found incomplete and fuzzy thinking. They simply had no defined idea. For the most part, they adopted an ambiguous definition of the most basic terms. This is common to most anyone you talk to on the subject. So, what then is the difference?

As with all things spiritual, the Bible is the *go-to* book for answers. In the first book of the Bible, we find the complete answer to the basic question:

"And the LORD God formed man *of* the dust of the ground, and breathed into his nostrils the breath of life; and man became a living soul." (Genesis 2:7 KJV)

Here we have the formula that makes man what he is. Physically formed out of the ground, animated by spirit, the first man became a living being. It is simple and straight forward in meaning. Just as the mathematical equation $1 + 2 = 3$, so in like manner body + spirit = soul.

First, we have the body which is made out of dirt, the organic building blocks of all carbon based living things. It is physical, temporal, and subject to its environment; we truly are fragile creatures. The requirements for physical sustainability are precise. It must have certain things such as air, nutrients, and a specific temperature range to survive. The body isn't immortal. It ages and deteriorates, often much sooner than we would like. In its early stages, it shows an affinity for growth and regeneration only to eventually wither and die, the result of man's transgression in the Garden of Eden.

To this dirt God injected the breath - spirit - of life. Throughout the Old Testament, the original Hebrew words rendered in English as spirit are NESHAMAH and RUACH, both of which carry the meaning of blowing or respiration, with only a slight difference between them. They are often paralleled, i.e. used interchangeably. In the Hebrew, there is no separate word for breath apart from spirit. Depending on the bias of the translator, the same words could be rendered either way. Literally, they mean wind, breath, or perhaps, more accurately, the movement of air. Abstractly, they convey the idea of animation; they indicate life. When we see a person's chest cavity move through the process of breathing, we know that they are alive.

The spirit in man reveals his character. When we speak breath leaves the body after passing through the vocal chords which create sound. Encoded within our breath and sound are our thoughts. Our spirit expresses our innermost thinking, and as it proceeds from out of us, therefore, it is the expression of our personality.

In the 1st chapter of the book of 1 Samuel, is the story of the birth of Samuel the Prophet and a great example of how it reveals one's character. His father had two wives, one of which, Peninnah, provided him with children, but Samuel's mother Hannah had been barren. This situation provided a source of irritation to her as his other wife used it as a reproach against her. As was customary, his parents made their yearly pilgrimage to Shiloh to sacrifice to the Lord. While they were there, Hannah, through her personal anguish, prayed silently to the Lord for a son. Though her lips were moving and her breath was leaving her body, she made no sound. Eli the High Priest noted her actions, thinking her lack of sound was due to drunkenness and rebuked her for his perceived lack of her sobriety. She responded to this by explaining that it was due to her *sorrowful spirit* (1:15). She was a sad person and the spirit/breath that proceeded from her revealed it.

The expression of who we are through the spirit happens because it indwells and explores the depths of our being. If something is in our thoughts, then our spirit is acquainted with it.

But, as it is written, "What no eye has seen, nor ear heard, nor the heart of man imagined, what God has prepared for those who love him"-- these things God has revealed to us through the Spirit. For the Spirit searches everything, even the depths of God. For who knows a person's thoughts except the spirit of that person, which is in him? So also no one comprehends the thoughts of God except the Spirit of God. (1 Corinthians 2:9-11)

The spirit is an information highway whereby all data can be processed and moved. Take the smartphones of today as an example. The very same cord used to charge up the phones battery can also ferry information from the phone to a computer or vice versa. This is how the Almighty One sees into the hearts of men.

> The spirit of man is the lamp of the LORD, searching all his innermost parts. (Proverbs 20:27)

God uses our spirit as a probe to see inside us. We can never deceive or fool Him in anything, for by our very own spirit He knows exactly what's going on in our thoughts. He is inescapable.

"To the choirmaster. A Psalm of David. O LORD, you have searched me and known me! You know when I sit down and when I rise up; you discern my thoughts from afar. You search out my path and my lying down and are acquainted with all my ways. Even before a word is on my tongue, behold, O LORD, you know it altogether. You hem me in, behind and before, and lay your hand upon me. Such knowledge is too wonderful for me; it is high; I cannot attain it. Where shall I go from your Spirit? Or where shall I flee from your presence? If I ascend to heaven, you are there! If I make my bed in Sheol, you are there! If I take the wings of the morning and dwell in the uttermost parts of the sea, even there your hand shall lead me, and your right hand shall hold me. If I say, "Surely the darkness shall cover me, and the light about me be night," even the darkness is not dark to you; the night is bright as the day, for darkness is as light with you. For you formed my inward parts; you knitted me together in my mother's womb." (Psalm 139:1-13)

While the spirit brings that spark of life which animates us and searches our innermost being, and while it demonstrates our character to those about us, it is nowhere indicated in the scriptures that our consciousness is bound up in it. Solomon, the writer of Ecclesiastes, made it clear that the dead are unaware of the mundane things that occupy the living:

"But he who is joined with all the living has hope, for a living dog is better than a dead lion. For the living know that they will die, but the dead know nothing, and they have no more reward, for the memory of them is forgotten. Their love and their hate and their envy have already perished, and forever they have no more share in all that is done under the sun." (Ecclesiastes 9:4-6)

"Turn, O LORD, deliver my life; save me for the sake of your steadfast love. For in death there is no remembrance of you; in Sheol who will give you praise?" (Psalm 6:4, 5)

"Put not your trust in princes, in a son of man, in whom there is no salvation. When his breath departs, he returns to the earth; on that very day his plans perish." (Psalm 146:3, 4)

As can be seen in the Psalm above, when a man's breath (spirit) leaves the body, the decay process of death begins and the thought process ends. The word translated as *plans* in the English Standard Version is the Hebrew ESHTONAH, used once only here in the Bible. It is derived from the root word ASHATH, meaning *to shine*. Many other versions render it as thoughts or thinking, the idea being as you develop a shine on something by rubbing it, so your thoughts are developed by the action of thinking. This process ends when the spirit separates from the body. James, the half-brother of Jesus and pastor of the Jerusalem church, touched upon this truth in his epistle:

For as the body apart from the spirit is dead, so also faith apart from works is dead. (James 2:26)

He readily asserts that death comes as a result of the separation of the spirit and flesh. At the parting of the two, all consciousness ceases. Any plans, thoughts, or desires no longer hold sway; the mind stops being aware of anything. As to the separateness of the mind and spirit, the venerable Apostle to the Gentiles, Paul, told the Church at Corinth that God's elect could know the mind of Him through the action of the Spirit:

"For who knows a person's thoughts except the spirit of that person, which is in him? So also no one comprehends the thoughts of God except the Spirit of God. Now we have received not the spirit of the world, but the Spirit who is from God, that we might understand the things freely given us by God. And we impart this in words not taught by human wisdom but taught by the Spirit, interpreting spiritual truths to those who are spiritual. The natural person does not accept the things of the Spirit of God, for they are folly to him, and he is not able to understand them because they are spiritually discerned. The spiritual person judges all things, but is himself to be judged by no one. "For who has understood the mind of the Lord so as to instruct him?" But we have the mind of Christ." (1 Corinthians 2:11-16)

Notice that he said the Spirit searches out and knows the thoughts of God, not that *it is* His mind. Paul understood it to be distinct from the consciousness of Him with whom we interact. It simply is an avenue and a source of power whereby information can be transferred back and forth; it gives life and movement to the flesh. Are we not wonderfully and fearfully made? This idea of consciousness apart from the spirit is further reinforced later in the same letter when he stated that he would rather pray with his mind *as well* as his spirit (1 Corinthians 14:14, 15). If our consciousness resides in our spirit, as many teach, how can we ignore passages such as these?

It is apparent that in our flesh we have cognitive powers, at least while we are awake. Yet, it is possible for one to be alive yet not conscious of their surroundings, as is often in sleep or a coma. If this awareness doesn't rest in the spirit, from where then does it come? It comes from the soul.

The soul is the sum total of man's existence. As it says in Genesis chapter 2, the first man was physically formed from the dust of the earth, injected with the breath of life, and thus became a living soul. The soul (Hebrew NEPHESH) is not a touchable thing, but is rather the action of being alive; it is a *state of being*. Therefore, to be a living soul one has to have a united body and spirit. These requirements are absolute. Apart from the body, the soul, and the consciousness that comes with it, just doesn't exist. There are many stories of people having died and ascended into heaven or descending into hell. They abound with descriptions of angels, demons, and even Jesus Himself. To be candid they are lies, whether the individuals telling them are just mistaken or purposely fabricating them.

The soul is not unique to mankind as some suppose and teach, but is the state of all living, breathing creatures. If it breaths and is alive, it is a soul. Thus, in the original Hebrew animals are spoken of as souls:

"So God created the great sea creatures and every *living creature* (Literally soul, NEPHESH) that moves, with which the waters swarm, according to their kinds, and every winged bird according to its kind. And God saw that it was good. And God blessed them, saying, "Be fruitful and multiply and fill the waters in the seas, and let birds multiply on the earth." And there was evening and there was morning, the fifth day. And God said, "Let the earth bring forth *living creatures* (NEPHESH) according to their kinds--livestock and creeping things and beasts of the earth according to their kinds." And it was so." (Genesis 1:21-24)

Because the soul is dependent on a united body and spirit it cannot exist by itself as a stand-alone entity. It is, therefore, definitely not immortal. The willingness of Bible teachers to call the soul immortal is misleading, whether intentional or not, and can be hazardous. We that teach God's word are held to a higher standard (James 3:1). It may come as a shock to those taught otherwise that the soul can and does die.

"Behold, all souls are mine; the soul of the father as well as the soul of the son is mine: the soul who sins shall die". (Ezekiel 18:4)

The soul that sins shall die. That means everyone, because all men, regardless of upbringing or status in this world, commit sin. God sees all men the same (Romans 3:21-23). This death, as any child who has attended Sunday school knows, was brought about in the Garden of Eden (Genesis chapter 3). Eve, the mother of all men, was approached by our adversary Satan, in the form of a serpent. Even though she knew through Adam that they were not permitted by the Creator to eat the fruit of the tree of knowledge of good and evil, she readily accepted the lie that he proffered, saying, "You shall not die." The Hebrew in that passage is quite clear and simple: He told her she would not die, and she bought it. To this day, mankind universally is buying in to the same deception. Even though they know that they will cease to be, they accept the lie that they will yet live, albeit in another form. The Satanic lie of an afterlife began with Eve in the Garden, its power stems from the redefining of the word, death.

That the soul literally dies can easily be seen by scripture; a more direct use of the word *die* cannot be employed. And, as if the literal is not enough in my own studies, I have discovered the use of the word *sleep* or one of its variants being used figuratively for death at least fifty-five times. Allegorically speaking, to die is to go to sleep. When we, as reasonably sound and healthy individuals, go to sleep, it is our hope to awaken the next morning. In God's great and beautiful plan, we die in hope of awaking in the resurrection of the righteous on the Day of the Lord. A more elegant and appropriate picture of this can't be found than that of the resurrection of Jesus. He was dead, lifeless as a block of wood, unconscious of all things, but He died in hope that God would not leave His soul in the state of non-existence.

As crude as this may sound to some, the concept of dying and going to heaven is a "pipe dream." Without even factoring in the basic truth concerning the temporal nature of the body, soul, and spirit of man, there is absolutely no *direct* evidence from the scriptures to support it. Nowhere does it say anything such as, "When you die you're going to heaven." There are, however, plenty of indirect passages of scripture that without the proper foundational definitions can be twisted to read as if they did. A few of the more popular arguments will be addressed to shed some spiritual and intellectual light on the matter. Remember, apart from the body, the soul does not exist. This is a most important foundational truth: The soul of man dies.

One of the most prevalent Biblical arguments for an afterlife concerns the thief on the cross. In my conversations, I've had people use this one as a proof text for the consensus view. During the crucifixion, Jesus told one of the thieves joining Him that he would "be with him in paradise that day" (Luke 23:43). It seems to be cut and dried. The problem with the argument (aside from the foundational truth mentioned above) comes from two things: The difference between Greek and English grammar, and the definition of the word *paradise*.

That so many accept this argument is to be understood. Those who have interpreted the passage in Luke have done so according to a bias toward an afterlife. Notice the difference between the two versions:

"And he said to him, "Truly, I say to you, today you will be with me in Paradise." (English Standard Version)

"And Jesus said to him, "Verily, to you am I saying today, with Me shall you be in paradise" (Concordant Literal New Testament)

While the ESV follows suit with the catholic interpolation, the Concordant Literal New Testament breaks rank and takes a lesser known but, I believe, a scripturally correct one. The universally taught afterlife bias makes Jesus to promise that the thief will enter His kingdom that very same day, whereas the correct Biblical perspective informs us that Jesus was telling the thief *on that very day* that he would indeed enter paradise with Him (at, as then, yet unknown time). It's all in the placement of a comma.

It must be understood by the lay person that Koine Greek syntax (sentence structure) is different from English. In English, syntax follows a basic formula based on word order; usually a noun precedes a verb, followed by the direct object. But in Greek, syntax is determined by word endings. The words themselves can be in any position. Add to this that there are no punctuation marks in the original Greek, and it then becomes easy to see how a translator can guide the reader to accept a certain position as being correct. Knowing that the soul is a perishable state of existence helps us to determine the true reading.

Theoretically, if the syntax wasn't an issue, and the nature of the soul wasn't temporal, we would still have a problem with the passage teaching an afterlife. This stems from the definition of *paradise*. It is assumed by the average person that it is just another name for heaven, of which it is not. It is actually a physical place found upon earth.

The etymology of paradise is interesting. It is believed by linguists to have originated in the Old Iranian language known as Avestan. It comes from a compound word: PAIRI = around and DAEZA = wall / brick, indicating a walled enclosure. It then found its way into the European languages through the Greek PARADIESOS. The Hebrew has an equivalent word, PARDACE, believed also to be borrowed from Avestan. The idea that the scriptures present of it, is that of an enclosed garden or park. The Garden of Eden was such a place. It was a protected place of ready sustenance with only one apparent entrance. When God expelled Adam and Eve from it they could not reenter because He placed an armed angel to guard its entrance

(Genesis 3:24). When the Jewish scholars translated the Old Testament into Greek (known as the Septuagint or LXX), it was the Greek PARADIESOS that they used for the Garden in Eden.

This tells us that paradise is an actual, protected place where nothing can enter uninvited. It existed thousands of years ago when God placed the first man there, but has since disappeared into obscurity. In Revelation 2:7, we see a promise given to those who conquer over evil to partake of the tree of life found *in the paradise* of God:

"He who has an ear, let him hear what the Spirit says to the churches. To the one who conquers I will grant to eat of the tree of life, which is in the paradise of God."

This tree is not found just anywhere, but has a specific place where it will grow: Within the safety of the enclosed paradise of God, the New Jerusalem.

"Then the angel showed me the river of the water of life, bright as crystal, flowing from the throne of God and of the Lamb through the middle of the street of the city; also, on either side of the river, the tree of life with its twelve kinds of fruit, yielding its fruit each month. The leaves of the tree were for the healing of the nations." (Revelation 22:1, 2)

Paradise does not as yet exist in this world, but is destined to thrive in the world to come. This is the true hope of all God's children: Resurrection into the coming kingdom of God. This is precisely why that thief on the cross next to Jesus could not have entered into His kingdom on the day that he died. His soul ceased to be and, figuratively speaking, he went to sleep until the day of resurrection, just as Jesus did, whose resurrection happened on the third day. That thief on the cross is today dead and in a grave somewhere awaiting the resurrection of the righteous. One can't go to paradise unless they have a body. In II Corinthians chapter 12: 1-4, Paul told of a man who had a vision and was taken to paradise and heard things that mortal man cannot repeat. As to the man's state, Paul said he didn't know if he was there in his body or not. The reason is simple: Paul knew by divine revelation that the paradise of God was yet a future event for those who are in the flesh.

Another argument many put forth for an afterlife says that, "To be absent from the body is to be present with the Lord." This is based on a text from II Corinthians 5:8, the meaning of which is certainly not understood properly. In order to have a clear view one must look to its context:

"For we know that if the tent that is our earthly home is destroyed, we have a building from God, a house not made with hands, eternal in the heavens. For in this tent we groan, longing to put on our heavenly dwelling, if indeed by putting it on we may not be found naked. For while we are still in this tent, we groan, being burdened--not that we would be unclothed, but that we would be further clothed, so that what is mortal may be swallowed up by life. He who has prepared us for this very thing is God, who has given us the Spirit as a guarantee. So we are always of good courage. We know that while we are at home in the body we are away from the Lord, for we walk by faith, not by sight. Yes, we are of good courage, and we would rather be away from the body and at home with the Lord. So whether we are at home or away, we make it our aim to please him. For we must all appear before the judgment seat of Christ, so that each one may receive what is due for what he has done in the body, whether good or evil." (2 Corinthians 5:1-10)

What Paul was telling the church at Corinth was that we as disciples of the Lord are dwelling in a temporary shelter, a tent, which is our natural flesh, and that God has prepared for us a permanent glorified house that is also spiritual in nature, our glorified body. Our natural inclination is to yearn for it, and as long as we are at home in our body, we are absent from Him. How? Spiritually?

No, we have His Spirit as a pledge of His promise of salvation (Ephesians 1:13, 14). We are absent from Him physically. This can only be remedied in the resurrection of the righteous when we see Him face to face, not in heaven when our body dies. Resurrection and judgment go hand in hand, and the language in the above text is mirrored in Romans chapter 8. Remember, the soul that sins will die. All men sin, so all will die.

But what about the Prophet Elijah? Did he not ascend into heaven in a whirlwind? That story from the 2nd chapter of II Kings is a staple of Sunday school lessons. Elijah, the great prophet that overthrew the 450 prophets of Baal (1 Kings Chapter 18) and who had raised the dead (1 Kings Chapter 17), handing over the mantle of authority to his successor Elisha so that he could go to be with God. But did he actually go to the spiritual realm? Absolutely not! That he was picked up by a whirlwind and taken up into the sky, there can be no doubt. It should be noted that the Hebrew language is concrete and not abstract. Both the sky above and the spiritual dwelling of God are indicated by the same word, SHAMAYIM. It can be used in either case. So, how do we know that Elijah was not taken into the spiritual throne room of the Almighty One?

Firstly, it is conceded by intellectually honest scholars that Elijah wrote a letter to King Jehoram of Judah some years after his whirlwind event (II Kings, chapter 2). This can be easily ascertained by observing the chronological reigns of the Judean and Israeli kings during that period. Elijah's last recorded act was to confront Israel's Ahaziah for his sins (II Kings, chapter 1). His tenure was very short lasting, about two years. He came to power in the seventeenth year of Jehoshaphat, King of Judah's, reign. Jehoshaphat ruled Judea for 25 years after which Jehoram took full control of the nation. Shortly after ascending to the throne, he had all his brothers killed to prevent them from any possible treason. It was upon that occasion that Elijah wrote a letter to rebuke his actions (II Chronicles 21:12-15). If he went to heaven, as is believed by many, then he couldn't have possibly written the letter.

Secondly, and more importantly, Jesus declared that no one has ever ascended up to heaven:

"No one has ascended into heaven except he who descended from heaven, the Son of Man" (John 3:13)

The occasion for that statement was His conversation with Nicodemus in which He witnessed to the fact that He was the Anointed One of God. To ascend to heaven is to attain immortality, something that even Jesus had to die for to achieve. For Elijah to bypass death is to negate the word of God that says that the soul that sins will die (Ezekiel 18:4), and that it is appointed unto all men to die once (Hebrews 9:27).

It is popularly taught among some groups that there are three heavens. This stems from the passage in II Corinthians 12:1-4, where Paul the Apostle told of a man who was caught up into the *third heaven*. Apart from that, there is no mention of a third heaven anyplace else in the scriptures. The conventional thinking is that the word heaven is represented by three separate places. The first place is the sky above us, where the birds fly and the clouds drift. The second is that area we call outer space, where the stars and planets find their home. The third is the spiritual dimension, where the Almighty God sits on His throne. This interpretation, while making sense, falls short of correctly identifying its use in the Bible.

The Hebrew word for heaven, SHAMAYIM, has a distinct meaning that is not properly reflected in English translations. Virtually all modern versions of the Bible render it in the plural, heavens, whereas the King James Version (long the standard in Biblical exegesis) renders it in the singular. Neither approach does justice to the original, however, due to the Hebrew having also a dual number, of which SHAMAYIM is representative. Literally, it refers to two heavens; the singular is unused in scripture. Thus, Genesis 1:1 tells us that God created the two heavens and the earth.

As stated above, the concept of a third heaven finds its basis in the New Testament's second letter to the church at Corinth:

"I must go on boasting. Though there is nothing to be gained by it, I will go on to visions and revelations of the Lord. I know a man in Christ who fourteen years ago was caught up to the third heaven-- whether in the body or out of the body I do not know, God knows. And I know that this man was caught up into paradise--whether in the body or out of the body I do not know, God knows-- and he heard things that cannot be told, which man may not utter." (2 Corinthians 12:1-4)

If it were not for these four verses, I scarcely believe that few, if any, would espouse the view that three is the exact number of heavens. A closer examination reveals that Paul equates the third heaven with paradise, which has its existence on the new earth. To determine the truth, there can be many angles from which we can approach these facts, but in order to make sense of it all, one matter that I believe must be addressed is that the present heavens are destined to be destroyed.

"But by the same word the heavens and earth that now exist are stored up for fire, being kept until the day of judgment and destruction of the ungodly." (II Peter 3:7)

"But the day of the Lord will come like a thief, and then the heavens will pass away with a roar, and the heavenly bodies will be burned up and dissolved, and the earth and the works that are done on it will be exposed." (II Peter 3:10)

God has determined a day yet in the future when He will make an end of all that exists before our human eyes. The writer of the book of Hebrews, quoting the 102nd Psalm, said that He will roll them (the foundations of the earth) up as a robe and as a garment they will wear out (Hebrews 1:10-12). That which is temporal will give way to that which is eternal. In the beginning, He created two heavens, one physical, the other spiritual. The second one is the spiritual realm. At the end of the Day of the Lord, He will destroy both to create a new "heaven" and earth where He will dwell among men.

"Then I saw a new heaven and a new earth, for the first heaven and the first earth had passed away, and the sea was no more. And I saw the holy city, new Jerusalem, coming down out of heaven from God, prepared as a bride adorned for her husband. And I heard a loud voice from the throne saying, "Behold, the dwelling place of God is with man. He will dwell with them, and they will be his people, and God himself will be with them as their God." (Revelation 21:1-3)

"Then the angel showed me the river of the water of life, bright as crystal, flowing from the throne of God and of the Lamb through the middle of the street of the city; also, on either side of the river, the tree of life with its twelve kinds of fruit, yielding its fruit each month. The leaves of the tree were for the healing of the nations. No longer will there be anything accursed, but the throne of God and of the Lamb will be in it, and his servants will worship him." (Revelation 22:1-3)

This new heaven and earth *is the third heaven.* The Almighty One, through the physical person of Jesus, will dwell with all men in a spiritual/material hybrid universe. No longer will the concrete and the abstract differ, but all things will be the same. The promise is given to us that we who conquer over the sin of this world will eat freely of the tree of life found in the paradise of God, the third heaven (Revelation 2:7).

Has anyone, other than Christ, since ascended into the spiritual realm? Yes! As Jesus told Nicodemus, "That which is born of the flesh is flesh, and that which is born of the Spirit is spirit" (John 3:6). He who was the firstfruits of the resurrection (1 Corinthians 15:20, 23) was the first human being to attain immortality. After His resurrection, there were some others who were reanimated (Matthew 27:52, 53). These were resurrected after Christ, but before the general resurrection of the righteous which will transpire at the beginning of the Day of the Lord. It is conceivable that they were present the day that Jesus ascended into the sky and may have went up with Him, for the angelic witnesses present testified that He would return in like manner (Acts 1:9-11), for upon His return He will be leading the saints (John 10:16; Revelation 19:11-14). He is the first one to cross that barrier between the spiritual and the material, and in the coming resurrection of the righteous on the Day of the Lord, we who are the elect of God will also partake of that eternal life.

HELL

The doctrine of hell and eternal punishment were for me difficult from which to escape. Unlike other doctrines that I changed my thinking on, it took me a couple of years to fully grasp the implications involved in it. It was for me, and is still for some, an assumed truth. I had been taught it all my life, and it was thoroughly implanted in my mind, and the thought of it being wrong just was not entertained.

It saddens me to a certain point when I reflect on the loss of certain songs I've associated with my walk of faith in this life. I can no longer sing some hymns in good conscience because I know their message is simply wrong. Being reared in the Missionary Baptist faith, I found a measure of comfort in singing *"When We All Get to Heaven"* only to discover that it (and many others) was at best based on an incorrect and unsubstantiated doctrine, that of an afterlife. Now, many years later, I'm firmly rooted in the doctrine of resurrection, not the "pie in the sky when you die" mentality that governs the majority of professing Christians. The other side of that coin is the doctrine of eternal punishment. It is the complement to a heavenly reward and the natural outgrowth of the belief in an afterlife.

The doctrine of hell and of an eternal punishment dishonors the Almighty One and is not worthy of being associated with His magnificent nature. Try as some may to prove its scriptural basis, it simply is not supported by God's word. He did not originate such teachings, and it must surely grieve His Spirit every time man attributes them to Him.

I slowly began to open my spiritual eyes to the fallacy of that teaching after I came to grips with the true nature of man. The formula is as simple as $1 + 2 = 3$: The body + the spirit = the soul. The soul of man is not a tangible thing, but is rather his state of being. It is the sum total of his existence. One Sunday morning several years ago, I taught this to the congregation at a Baptist church where my wife and I belonged. It was well received by those who were in attendance that day, at least no one openly disagreed with what I imparted. However, at the evening service, an elderly gentleman approached thanking me for that morning's lesson, but expressed confusion over the definition of the soul. He showed me a passage from Matthew 10:28, where Jesus said *"And fear not them which kill the body, but are not able to kill the soul: but rather fear him which is able to destroy both soul and body in hell."* If the soul, he reasoned, was able to survive the death of the body and exist in a perpetual state of torment, how could it die? I was taken aback. All I could do was admit I didn't fully understand all there was to know about the subject. At that time, I was convinced that the foundational teaching on the soul's properties was correct, but I'd not even considered how the doctrine of eternal punishment tied into it or even if it was in error. I was then faced with a challenge: How to reconcile the truth about man's nature and how to explain what the Bible says about hell.

It may seem cynical to some, but over the years I've learned to verify that which men profess to be God's word. This includes the translations of the original languages in which the scriptures were written. I've observed over the years that translators can and do twist the meaning of the Biblical text at times. This is not to accuse anyone of malfeasance, but to introduce the idea that bias is universal; it's all a matter of perception. I'm certainly no linguist, my Greek and Hebrew are rudimentary at best and I struggle with my own native English language well enough, but I've come to believe that if one is willing and has faith in God's purpose in this life, He is faithful to direct us into all truth. Therefore, I always as much as I can look into how words are used throughout the Bible to ascertain what the writers originally intended to express.

The doctrine of eternal punishment did not come to us through the Hebrew faith; it is pagan in its origin. The paradigm for it is evident in the mythology of the Greeks. Based upon the idea of an afterlife (the lie which began in the Garden of Eden, Genesis 3), it was employed by the ancient authorities (both secular and religious) as a way of keeping the ignorant masses in line by inducing a fear of non-ending torture. The Greek historian Polybius (c. 200-118 B.C.E.) was of this opinion, believing that the present practice of his day was counterproductive to civic progress. In his *The Histories,* he wrote concerning the Roman authorities that, "For this reason I think, not that the ancients acted rashly and at haphazard in introducing among the people notions concerning the gods and beliefs in the terrors of hell, but that the moderns are most rash and foolish in banishing such beliefs." (Hist. 6:56.12) Based upon the Hebrew Bible, the Jews had no such superstition.

There is an opinion among a great many scholars that hell and eternal punishment was not developed as a doctrine until just before the time of Christ, and that the early writings are silent in its regard. While I agree that the subject is not broached often, it is still there, but not widely recognized because it stands in opposition to what the majority of scholars *want* to believe. As with all other things, the simplest answer is usually the best.

In the Hebrew Scriptures, the word SHEOL is used as the *place* of the dead. It comes from the root שאל SH'AL, which indicates the action of requiring or asking. It appears that the significance of the root is that SHEOL requires or asks for the souls of men. Hebrew, being a concrete language, relates to the five senses, and the soul of man is thought of in terms of being a thing; something that, though not seen, yet exists. At death, all souls are relegated to a common dark destiny that asks for them, SHEOL. The body also goes to the place that asks for it (Genesis 42:38). On a physical level, SHEOL can be the grave or just a hole in the ground (Numbers 16:30), whereas in a figurative sense the soul (which is actually not a thing but a *state of being*) is relegated to its place. This is the word that is designated in English translations as hell.

It is a fact that people are going to view things according to their own particular bias. If you have been trained in a certain doctrine, you more often than not will see everything as relating to that point of view. It is a sad and unfortunate truth, but it is not true in all cases. Through perseverance and a willingness to pursue truth, one can overcome their personal shackles and attain the freedom of genuine enlightenment. Bible translators are no different. When they translate a word such as SHEOL into a language that has no exact equivalent, misunderstandings can and do occur often as a result of their bias. SHEOL has no equivalent in Western thought and culture. How then did this Hebrew word come to be associated with an eternal fiery prison of torture?

The Bible is a Hebrew book written by men who lived in a specific Eastern culture. Their manner of thinking and writing differs from modern Western culture, which is heavily influenced by Grecian philosophy and language, and although the New Testament was written in Greek, its author's mindset was Hebraic. This can be problematic as Christianity has become a largely Gentile or non-Jewish faith. What has happened is that the church (in the collective sense) has strayed from its Hebrew based faith through Greek philosophy and language.

In the New Testament, the words translated as hell are HADES and GEHENNA. HADES is strictly a Greek word which was used in their mythology to designate the god of the underworld, Hades. It actually came to refer to the entire underworld itself, which was divided into two parts: the Elysian Fields, a blissful place for the heroic and virtuous souls of the dead, and Tartarus, an inescapable gloomy deep place of eternal torments. GEHENNA, however, is a transliterated Hebrew word for a place: The valley of Ben Hinnom, an ancient place of pagan sacrifice. It is a compound of GHEE (Greek for *land*), and the name Hinnom. These two are designated by most translators by the same English word hell. They are in fact two distinct words with two separate meanings that should never receive the same treatment.

HADES is the equivalent to SHEOL in that it refers to the abode of the deceased. Physically it is the grave (Acts 2:27). Figuratively, it is the state of oblivion, non-existence. It is used just 11 times in the New Testament, only 5 of which were by Jesus. The scarcity of its use should be an alarm to expositors and preachers who see the importance to frequently teach on the subject. In its use, it is not associated in any way with fire or torment, except in one allegorical passage.

In Luke 16:19-31 is the story of Lazarus and the Rich Man. Long thought of by many as a literal account rather than a parable of what happens to the soul of man after death, it has become a source of misinformation, some even developing doctrine from it. To take it literally, however, is very unwise because it is simply a parable that Jesus aimed at the faithless religionists of His day. He had a message to preach that they *should* have accepted and embraced.

The message of Jesus, called the Gospel (meaning good news), was the heralding of the coming kingdom of God (Mark 1:14; Matthew 4:17). It was what He preached all the days of His ministry, and it was given to His followers to continue the work. The responsibility of preserving and proclaiming the Gospel of the kingdom was originally given to the nation of Israel; they were to be a light and example to the world. It, however, became a perfunctory exercise lacking faith in the Almighty One (Romans 9:29-32). Faithfulness to the work of preaching the Gospel was the occasion for the teaching of the parable. As with any other passage in the Bible, the context is important to a correct interpretation. In the three preceding chapters (14-16) before the parable, everything Jesus uttered had a common thread running through it: Stewardship. There are a total of ten parables that He used to the edification of His disciples and the condemnation of His predecessors, the Pharisees, each one declaring a facet of that for which they were responsible. Through the law covenant, Israel became the administrators of God's kingdom business. It was incumbent on them to present the Law, which pointed to the Christ to the rest of the world and encouraged faith in God and His kingdom.

It begins with an invitation to dine at the house of a religious dignitary (14:1). During the course of the meal, Jesus heals a man afflicted with some form of water induced swelling (dropsy) in the presence of some Pharisees. This happening on a Sabbath brings about un-vocalized indignation, and Jesus, knowing their reverence for the ceremonial, used it to teach on the mercy of God. The text sets forth the dynamics involved: The Pharisees who were the representatives of the Law of Moses (Matthew 23:2, 3) were primarily concerned with keeping it to the letter. Jesus raises the question of which is more important, the letter of the Law or its underlying spiritual meaning. The groundwork for the Lazarus parable is laid for this beginning in the 14th chapter of Luke.

While dining, Jesus addresses the other guests, among whom were a number of Pharisees (14:7, 15:3), His host (14:12), a large crowd that followed Him (14:25), and lastly, His own disciples (16:1), which is the direct context. He teaches them a parable about shrewd management of temporal means which touches an exposed nerve with the Pharisees who had a penchant for wealth (16:14). Their ridicule of Jesus' words prompts Him to expound on the virtue of faithfulness, which launches the parable of Lazarus.

The illustration is actually quite simple once the main characters are correctly identified. There are three, Abraham, Lazarus, and the Rich Man. Abraham is not meant to be taken as an individual. He as the father of the faithful represents the election of God, His chosen ones who by faith will inherit the kingdom. Lazarus, which is the Hellenized form of the Hebraic Eliezer, was the head gentile servant of Abraham, who upon the birth of Isaac, received no material inheritance; he represents the Gentile nations. The Rich Man who had five brothers represented the tribe of Judah (who had five brothers, Genesis 29; 31-35; 30:17-20), of which the Pharisees were the spiritual leaders.

Abraham is the one with whom God made His covenant with mankind. He is called the father of many nations, and through him some peoples of all nations of the earth will find the blessing of an everlasting kingdom. This truth was obscured through time and the Jewish Pharisees, who were given the responsibility of preserving and disseminating the Gospel of God's coming Kingdom, were largely given over to the gaining of temporal treasures to gain and keep control of the poor and ignorant masses. Jesus spoke of this in the days before His crucifixion (Matthew 23). Originally, Abraham had no children and his substance, including the promises made to him by God, to his way of thinking, would have gone to his Gentile servant, Eliezer of Damascus, but God said to him that he would not be his heir and that he will have a son of his own. This was fulfilled in Isaac. In a literal sense, Abraham's Jewish offspring did receive a temporal kingdom upon the earth.

Because the Jews failed to serve the Lord through their lack of faith, He took away from them the Kingdom and its present business of preaching and gave it to the Gentile nations (Matthew 21:43). The Jews, who were the natural heirs (Rich Man), being tormented, were now cast out of the Kingdom and the Gentile believers (Lazarus) are finding rest in the promise given to the elect (Abraham). The Pharisees were not good stewards of the gift of the Kingdom. This is the meaning of the parable that so many have taken to be a literal account.

It is in conjunction with the other word, GEHENNA, where fire is mentioned (Matthew 5:22, 29, 30; 10:28, 18:9; Mark 9:43, 45, 47; James 3:6). It is found in only twelve verses, and, unlike HADES, it is never used as an equivalent to SHEOL, which is the state of non-existence, but rather is treated as an actual place into which one can be cast (Matthew 5:29, 30; 18:9; Luke 12:5), be destroyed (Matthew 10:28), and judged (Matthew 23:33). In no place do the scriptures say that anyone is *cast* into HADES. GEHENNA, therefore, is a description of a literal place of final judgment; the lake of fire of Revelation chapter 20 is the final judgment into which HADES and death are cast.

The two words, HADES and GEHENNA, are often erroneously translated in the English versions by the single word hell. A few of the modern versions do transliterate SHEOL and HADES in an effort to stay neutral, yet the common consensus among professing Christians is that hell is an eternal place of fiery punishment. This condition begs the question: Why would a loving God create such a place with such a manner of retribution?

Probably the most prevalent answer that I have received from its adherents is that God doesn't send men there, they send themselves. In my early years, I used that logic myself. But this does not begin to answer the question. Surely in His omniscience, He knew that some men would reject His offer of life and that they would be resigned to that fate, so why create a destination like that? It seems that the most common riposte to that inquiry is that He created it as a repository for Satan and his minions (Matthew 25:41). But then why allow men to go there? What purpose would it serve? The common replies to the question of how it could exist all fall short of a viable and adequate answer.

Modern Evangelicals often use the threat of an eternal death in a fiery blast furnace as an inducement to acceptance of God's salvation. This can follow two paths, one active and the other passive.

The active approach is when the teaching presents hell as a terrible place for the unrepentant sinner. It is often portrayed as a place of non-ending pain where the sinner is hopelessly trapped and the misery never lightened. The sinner is told that unless they repent and accept Christ they will perish forever in torment and get what they certainly deserve. The goal of this tactic is to actively scare the sinner into accepting God's salvation and save their own skin. I have heard this inducement preached from pulpits with my own ears.

The passive line of attack, while leaning on the doctrine of an eternal hell, takes a less aggressive approach. Instead of magnifying the sinner's faults, the emphasis is placed upon God's love for them and His desire for their escape. The fires of hell are still painted with bold brush strokes so that the prospective convert can see its torments. They are not actively cajoled or bullied into accepting Christ, but are passively led away from the precipice of destruction. I have witnessed this method as well.

The problem with both is that they rely upon fear as a stimulus to acceptance. This in itself is ineffectual to bringing about true repentance.

Whoever confesses that Jesus is the Son of God, God abides in him, and he in God. So we have come to know and to believe the love that God has for us. God is love, and whoever abides in love abides in God, and God abides in him. By this is love perfected with us, so that we may have confidence for the day of judgment, because as he is so also are we in this world. **There is no fear in love, but perfect love casts out fear. For fear has to do with punishment, and whoever fears has not been perfected in love.** (I John 4:15-18)

When we come to God for salvation it cannot be out of fear of retribution, but only through love. Consider for a moment the relationship between two people. Suppose you wanted an individual to love and desire to be with you. Would you hold a gun on them or some other form of emotional coercion and demand that they fall in love with you? And if it were possible that they did as a result of that, is that really what you'd want? Of course not! Would you not rather have them love and accept you out of their own genuine desire? You would prefer to have that person accept you of their own freewill, for then you would know that their love is true, and the Creator of all that exists is no different in that respect; after all, we were made in His image (Genesis 1:26).

It is the capacity for love that He endowed us with that set us apart from the rest of creation, and, while I cannot look into the hearts of those who profess to have come to Christ, I must confess that I have doubt that such an approach can yield anything positive or good. Does this doctrine in any way honor the true loving God that wishes that all men should come to repentance (II Peter 3:9)? Does it not tell the unregenerate sinner that He is a God of hateful vengeance who can eternally exist with the knowledge that men are suffering in an *unending* torment? He affirms that He loves us and wants us to enjoy an existence of bliss, but if we fail to comply He will allow us to suffer forever and ever. Does this in any way make the slightest sense?

There is an argument that says that God is not only a God of love, but also one of righteousness; that His righteous nature requires it. Such thinking just doesn't wash. While I certainly agree that the nature of God is set apart and righteous and evil cannot dwell with Him (Psalm 5:4), it presupposes that man has an eternal soul. The scriptures are clear: The soul that sins dies (Ezekiel 18:4, 20). Only if this truth is denied can such a doctrine be established. If God is in fact holy and righteous and evil cannot dwell with Him, then why and how could He eternally exist in a universe with a non-ending repository for aberrant beings?

The universal and commonly accepted concept of hell is false and incendiary (pun not intended) to the truth of God's merciful nature. It dishonors Him and hardens it's holder to un-Christ like behavior and attitudes. We are admonished to be like Him and not exhibit hate or retribution against others (1 Peter 2:23). How often have we expressed the idea that some individual deserves to go to hell, or after death experience the unending torments for things they have done? Such thinking and attitude is wrong and not worthy of those who have been redeemed and their expression an evident token that one is not walking worthy of their precious calling (Ephesians 4:1).

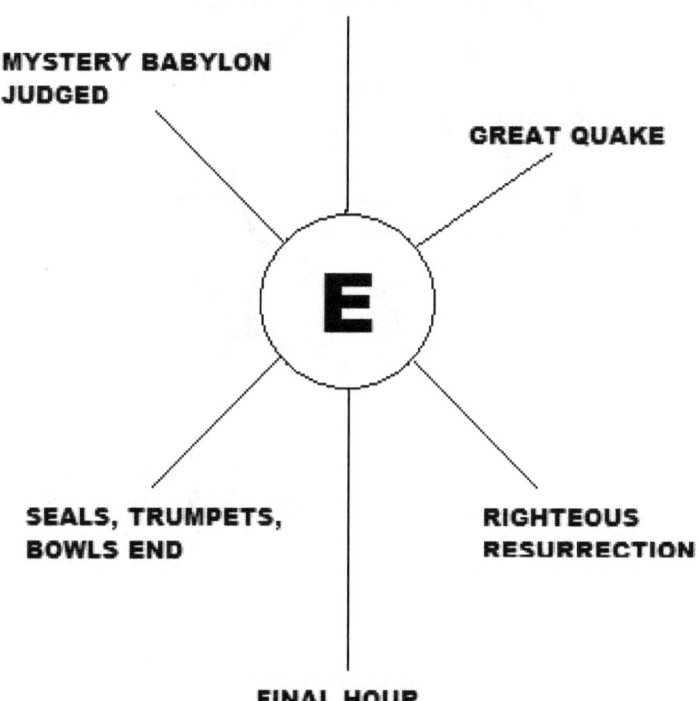

FIG. 1

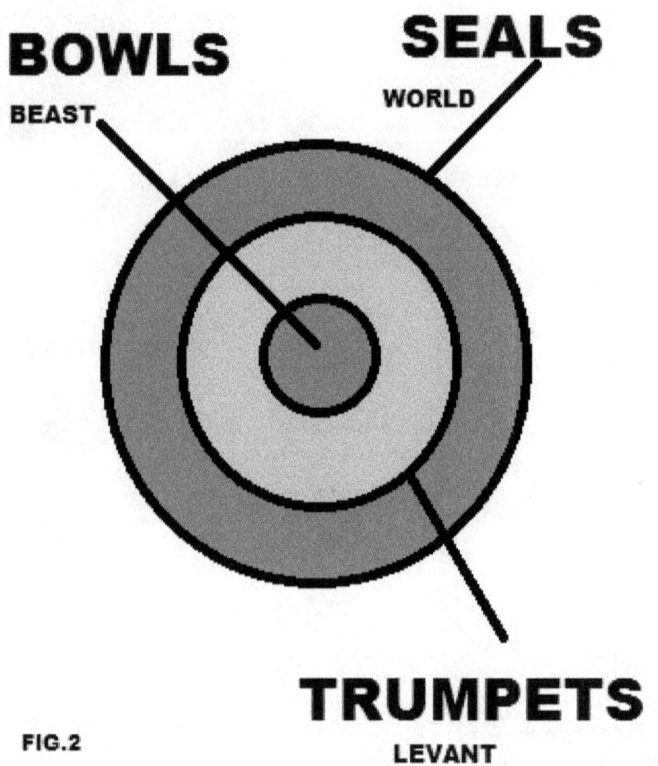

FIG.2

NOTES

1. 1Corinthians 2:14; "The natural person does not accept the things of the Spirit of God, for they are folly to him, and he is not able to understand them because they are spiritually discerned." natural person= Greek PSUCHIKOS, adjective form of PSUCHE, "SOUL". Man's actions are governed either by God's Spirit (Holy Spirit) or by his fleshly being; his soul. Jesus recognized this truth so His parables were aimed at those who had God's Spirit within them.
2. The probability that John was a priest is seemingly supported by several things.
   - At the last supper he sat next to Jesus, a seat traditionally saved for members of the priesthood (John 13:23-25).
   - Taking the position that the disciple whom John does not name is himself, during Jesus' interrogation at the house of Caiaphas he gained access by being known by the high priest (John 18:15).
   - There are a few allusions to the Temple services in the book of Revelation.
3. The Assyrian in Messianic Prophecy, Anthony Buzzard, first written May 9th 1986, edited Oct. 2001
4. Daniel David Luckenbill, Ancient Records of Assyria and Babylonia, Vol. II (University of Chicago Press, 1926, Greenwood Press Reprint, 1968). Section 784, p. 296 & section 909, 351.

INDEX

ABADDON, *Gk. Apollyon, Destructor,* 45, 47

ABYSSOS, *45*

AEON, *Gk. Age,* 19

AIONIOS, *Gk. Adjective form of AEON,* 19

ANTICHRIST, *Beast, man of sin,* 29, 31, 42, 53, 54, 98, 100-1, 103-6, 108-9, 111, 113, 121, 149

AORIST, *Gk. tense indicating completed action,* 64, 65

ARK OF THE COVENANT, 57, 107, 122-23, 125-132

ARMY OF GOD, *121, 122, 124, 125, 147*

ASSYRIAN, *86-102, 113, 131*

ASSYRIAN VIEW, (AV), *24*

BARFIELD, JIM, *108, 109*

BEAST, *Antichrist,* 26,31-4,38,42,53,98,100-19,134,142,144-5,147,153,160-2,167,168

BOQER, *Heb. Morning,* 16-17

BOWLS OF WRATH, *19, 25, 27, 31, 35, 40, 46, 51*

BULLSEYE, *seat of the Beast*, 26

BRIDE OF CHRIST, *144, 155*

CATHOLICISM, *universal dogma*, 71-2, 74

CHARACTER SKETCHES, *25, 29, 59 ,91*

CLIMAX, *25, 27-8, 48-50, 54, 59-60, 76, 133, 142*

COPPER SCROLLS, *125-6*

COPPER SCROLL PROJECT, *127*

DATIVE CASE, *use of preposition EN*, 13

DANIEL'S 70TH WEEK, *31-2,*

DART BOARD, *26*

DAY, *Hebraic concept of, 16, 17*

DAY OF THE LORD, *5, 12-19, 22-5, 27-31, 48, 50, 55-7, 59-60, 62, 65, 80-1, 83, 85, 88, 109, 111, 141-3, 149, 163-4, 168-70, 174-5, 177, 187, 195-61*

DEAD SEA SCROLLS, *125*

DRAGON, *Satan, 26, 53, 60, 93-8, 101*

"E", *focal point, 12-13, 15, 22*

EARTHQUAKE, GREAT, *27, 29, 47-8, 55-8, 62, 91, 138-42*

ECHAD, *Heb. One, 17*

EKKLESIA, *Gk. called out assembly, church, 66*

EN, *Gk. Preposition, in, among, 13*

EMEK HA MELEK, *valley of the king, 126*

EREV, *Heb. Evening, 16*

EUPHRATES, *26-7, 51-4, 150-1*

FALSE PROPHET, *Issa (Arabic Jesus), 26, 53, 60, 100-1, 106, 108, 119, 133, 142, 158*

FIRSTFRUITS, *82, 84, 166, 196*

FIVE SIGNS, *29, 56*

GEHENNA, *Heb. Valley of Ben Hinnom, 174, 201-2, 205-6*

GOG, *109, 117-18, 161, 167, 169*

HADES, *Gk. unseen, 39, 201-2, 206*

HOUR, FINAL, 51, 58, 102, *135-40, 146, 160, 162*

ISSA, *Arabic form of Jesus, 106, 108, 119, 158*

JIGSAW PUZZLE ILLUSTATION, *9*

KINGDOM OF GOD, *11-13, 28, 56-7, 59, 66-7, 72, 75, 83, 85-6, 111, 139-40, 173, 177, 188, 190, 203, 205*

KING OF ASSYRIA, *109-10, 112, 116-7*

KING OF BABYLON, *109, 112, 118*

KING OF THE NORTH, *32, 53, 159*

KING OF THE SOUTH, *32, 53-4, 159*

KHIRBET QUMRAN, *125, 127*

LAST DAY, *21-23, 168*

LEVANT VIEW, (LV), *31*

LIGHT, *defined as day,* 16, 23

LIGHT, GREAT, *over Jerusalem,* 19, 20, 143, 168, 170, 175

MAHDI, *Islamic messiah,* 32, 46-7, 104, 106, 119, 136, 150, 156-9, 162

MESSIAH, *Heb. anointed one,* 38, 105, 111-12, 146-47, 170-73

MISHKAN, *Heb. Tabernacle,* 107, 122, 124-27, 129

MYSTERY, BABYLON, *58, 144, 150-51, 153*

MYSTERY OF GOD, *12, 13, 15, 57, 75, 85-86*

NICOLAITANS, *69-71, 76*

NEBUCHADNEZZAR, *102, 124*

ORGEE, *Gk. wrath, 33*

ORTHODOXY, *71, 111*

PAROUSIA, *Gk. appearing, presence, 54, 177*

PLOT, *action of Revelation, 24, 26, 27, 56, 59, 79*

RAPTURE, *29, 46, 77, 136*

RESURRECTION, *21-23, 28, 57-59, 78, 83-84, 88, 91, 136, 145, 165-166, 168, 170, 173, 187, 190, 192, 196-197*

SCENE CHANGE RULE, *56, 133-34, 147-48*

SEAL(S), *24-29, 31, 33, 35, 39, 43, 47, 50, 55-56, 65, 79, 104, 140, 142, 145, 147*

SEAL OF GOD, *45-46, 80-82, 133*

SEVEN STEPS, *28-29, 31, 51*

SHEKINAH GLORY, *20, 143*

SHEMA, *Heb. hear, 6, 73*

SHEOL, *Heb. Abode of the dead, 74, 183-4, 200-02, 206*

SINGLE PERSPECTIVE, 5, *11*

SNELLEN EYE CHART, *12, 22*

TABERNACLE, *20, 107, 122-25, 127*

TARTARUS, *Gk. pit, in mythology lowest depth of Hades, 45, 202*

TERRITORIAL SPIRITS, *51, 103*

THE TWO WITNESSES, *29, 33, 60, 89, 91, 98, 161*

THIRD TEMPLE, *120-132*

THIRTEEN SUBPLOTS, *59-60*

THUMOS, *Gk. wrath, 33, 147*

TOWER OF BABEL, *75, 151-53*

TRIBULATION, GREAT, *12, 16, 28, 46, 49, 55-57, 60, 65, 77, 80, 82, 84, 91, 98, 131, 133-35, 137, 139, 145, 147, 149, 162*

TRUMPETS, *24-28, 31-2, 34, 37-8, 41-2, 45, 47, 51, 53, 55-6, 59, 145, 147*

TRUMPET, SEVENTH, *13, 29, 56, 58, 85-6, 90, 133*

WHITE THRONE JUDGMENT, *22, 169, 174, 177*

WHORE OF BABYLON, *149-50, 153, 155-57, 164*

WOMAN, HEAVENLY, *93-99, 102, 105, 149-50, 175*

WORLD VIEW (WV), *31*

www.ingramcontent.com/pod-product-compliance
Lightning Source LLC
Chambersburg PA
CBHW071453040426

42444CB00008B/1320